Tikal Report No. 23C

MISCELLANEOUS INVESTIGATIONS IN CENTRAL TIKAL: THE PLAZA OF THE SEVEN TEMPLES

University Museum Monograph 147

Tikal Report No. 23C

MISCELLANEOUS INVESTIGATIONS IN CENTRAL TIKAL: THE PLAZA OF THE SEVEN TEMPLES

H. Stanley Loten

Series Editors
William A. Haviland
Simon Martin

Published by

UNIVERSITY OF PENNSYLVANIA MUSEUM
of Archaeology and Anthropology
Philadelphia
2018

CATALOGING-IN-PUBLICATION DATA IS ON FILE WITH THE LIBRARY OF CONGRESS

ISBN 13: 978-1-934536-95-7
ISBN 10: 1-934536-95-4

Distributed for the University of Pennsylvania Museum of Archaeology and Anthropology
by the University of Pennsylvania Press.

Printed in the United States of America on acid-free paper.

Table of Contents

Tables

Illustrations

Editors' Note

Tikal Reports present the results of the University of Pennsylvania excavations from 1956–1969, largely in accord with the projected scheme set out by William R. Coe and William A. Haviland in Tikal Report 12. A great deal of research has taken place at Tikal since those investigations were completed with, in particular, several important projects undertaken by the Instituto Nacional de Antropología e Historia de Guatemala and the Agencia Española de Cooperación Internacional. Since their work has often enlarged upon that conducted by the University of Pennsylvania,—in some cases excavating the same structures—there is a clear opportunity to integrate recent and historical investigations to produce a synthetic treatment. This idea is undoubtedly appealing, but it is one we have resisted for the monograph series. The reasons are threefold. Firstly, consistency of scope and presentation was integral to the original scheme and has been implemented in all the reports published thus far. Secondly, the

Tikal Report authors do not have access to the newly produced data to anything like the extent necessary to do that work justice. Thirdly, to produce synthetic treatments of this kind would introduce very considerable delays in publishing future Tikal Reports, hampering the work of those scholars and students who could make immediate use of the data they contain. In acknowledgment of subsequent work, the introduction to each volume in the series will henceforth note where later work has taken place on the same structures and reference the relevant publications. Even without the addition of new data, the Tikal Report series provides needed information on things that can no longer be observed first hand, either because of excavation or continuing destruction by the elements.

William A. Haviland
Simon Martin
Series Editors

Abbreviations

Alt.: Altar
Bm.: Beam
Chm.: Chamber
Dr.: Door/Doorway
E: East
Fl.: Floor
FS.: Facade Sculpture
N: North
Rm.: Room
S: South
Ss.: Subspring
St.: Stela
Str.: Structure
W: West

Selected Architectural Terms

Note: These are just a few terms that occur in this volume. Some are new, others perhaps just not in general use in the Tikal series.

Aggregate
In concrete small stones or gravel are essential as stuff that the cement can stick to. Without aggregate concrete is mere grout with little strength as a mass.

Basal Platform
A substructure body exclusively sustaining a lower substructure platform.

Batter
Non-vertical faces are battered. Leaning outward is negative batter, inward is positive.

Beam
A spanning member is a beam. Wood beams are common but stone ones are known, particularly as lintels.

Building
The part of a structure that stands on a building platform and contains accessible rooms.

Building Platform
A building platform anticipates the plan of the building and provides a basis for the walls (see also "Fake Building Platform," below).

Butt
The parts of beams that bear on their supports are their butts. Some butts are concealed, others exposed.

Construction Stage
Major works of architecture at Tikal display a standard set of the following features: basal platform, pyramid, lower substructure platform, supplementary platform, building platform, building, and roofcomb. Building and building platform appear most frequently, and others appear on various structures in various combinations. They are numbered from topmost to basal, but described in reverse order, that is, basal to topmost. Although the terms imply distinct stages of construction, this is not always the case. For example, some building platforms are not stages of construction at all, and many buildings present walls, vaults, and upper zones as distinct constructional modules that perhaps might best be designated as substages, though this has not been formalized.

Capstone
Stones bridging the gap between half-vaults are capstones. Wood members bridging half-vault gaps are known and may be described as wooden capstones.

Cord Holder
Recessed pegs to which cords could be tied, usually found in interior wall faces flanking doorway openings, often in sets of four.

Epicentral Tikal
This term refers to the parts of the city center that are interconnected by continuous plaster paving. The nine structures described in this volume are all within it. Individual location maps for each structure depict part of epicentral Tikal. By means of the causeway system, the epicenter extends from the Great Plaza to the North Group and to Great Temple VI. Since plaster paving is inherently frag-

ile, maintaining such an extensive paving must have been important and meaningful.

Fake Building Platform

Beginning in Middle Classic times at Tikal, and evident only in certain structures, the building platform is no more than a series of moldings at the foot of exterior building wall faces. In some cases, this is obvious; in others, the building platform image is entirely convincing and requires excavation to show its true nature. It may be that many Late Classic Tikal structures display apparent building platforms that appear to support walls, but in fact are no more than exterior facade treatments.

Falsework

A timber structure set up during construction to establish lines, angles, and heights. Evidence consists only of socket holes.

Half-vault

From Intermediate through the Late Classic at Tikal vaults were installed by halves, first on one side of a room and then for completion, on the other side. The two half-vaults do not touch or lean against each other; each is independently stable. Short end-vault units prevent the long half-vaults from rolling into the room space.

Header

A facing stone set with its length projecting into the hearting of the wall or other feature.

Jamb

The sides of doorway openings are called jambs.

Lintel

A beam over a doorway, window, or niche is a lintel beam. Most lintels at Tikal employ a number of beams, many seemingly much too small in diameter for the load imposed by the vault mass and they must have been braced until vault mortar had reached full set.

Lower Substructure Platform

A number of structures consist of a building, a building platform, and a lower substructure platform that does not conform to definitions for supplementary platforms, pyramids, or basal platforms. These are designated simply as lower substructure platforms.

Medial Molding

At wall-top level a corbel course projecting out over the exterior wall surface is known as a medial molding.

Outset

Terraces, walls, and roofcombs, often have elements of surface projected out from other elements. Some may have iconographic significance, particularly rear axial outsets and stair-side outsets. Even side outsets might have carried meanings that would have been known to the people using the structures.

Preplastered

Workers sometimes applied plaster to masonry units prior to setting them in place. This is seen only on capstones in Late Classic construction and hence they provide a reliable diagnostic to this era at Tikal.

Range

Rooms of a building arranged with their length perpendicular to the structure axis constitute a "range." This is the basis of the term "range-type structure." Some range-type structures have more than one range set one in front of the other.

Rear Axial Outset

Certain structures have axial outsets in their rear facades, designated as rear axial outsets. These do not appear to serve any structural function and are not accessible as ledges on which persons might stand. They seem to have some significance in themselves, and they correlate with a definite set of other architectural features that may define temples.

Return Face

This term applies to facets of exterior surface that run perpendicular to the general orientation of facades—for example, end elements of outsets.

Riser

The vertical interval from tread to tread on a stair is a riser.

Rod Row

A series of small holes usually found immediately below a medial molding or a vault spring is known as a rod row. These holes are castes left by dowels only a few centimeters in diameter.

Roofcomb

A superstructure body, not supplied with accessible rooms, erected on a roof.

Rope Anchor

This is a fitting similar to a cord holder but much larger.

Socket

The hole left by a rotted out beam is a socket.

Soffit

The under-surface of a projecting member is its soffit. Vault surfaces over a room are soffit surfaces.

Spall

Small stones that occur in masonry joints and beds are spalls. Some may have been placed so as to provide a correct setting for the blocks, others may have been included in the mortar.

Stair-side Outset

Terrace outsets flanking stairs are known as stair-side outsets.

Stair-Side Ramp

Some outset stairs present sheer edges, while others have a slightly raised ramp-like edge, also known by the terms "*alfarda*" and balustrade.

Standing Architecture

Tikal ruins include many architectural structures only partially collapsed. Project operations cleared debris away from many of these, but others were left as originally found. These are known as examples of standing architecture and were recorded without removal of collapsed material or vegetation.

Stretcher

A facing stone set with its length running in the plane of the surface.

Subapron

Apron profiles at Tikal are of two main types: two-element aprons and three-element aprons. The two-element type typifies Early Classic work and consists of an upper part projecting over a lower part; the lower part is the subapron. This implies that the upper part is the apron, although the term "apron" is also applied to the whole feature whether two element or three element. In three-element aprons the subapron is the middle part.

Subspring Beam

Beams spanning rooms and set below vault spring height are subspring beams.

Substructure

The parts below the building are known collectively as the substructure.

Supplementary Platform

A substructure body intervening between a lower substructure platform and a building platform.

Tread

The horizontal part of a stair between risers is a tread.

Upper Zone

The exterior element corresponding to the vaults and overhanging exterior wall faces is the upper zone.

Vault

Masonry constructions that span over rooms or chambers are vaults. The vaults at Tikal are unlike arches in that one side does not depend on the other, they do not exert lateral thrusts, and do not require buttresses.

Vault-back

Some vaults have outer surfaces underlying upper zone material; these are known as vault-back surfaces. Some vaults at Tikal do not have vault-backs but most do.

Vault Beam

All known vaults at Tikal contain either wood beams, beam butts, or beam sockets. The beams are known as vault beams and in many cases were installed prior to masonry work as part of falsework and/or formwork. The way that vault soffit stones were cut around beams shows that the beams were in place first.

Veneer Facings

Facing stones proportioned so that their height is

distinctly greater than their thickness are known as veneer stones.

Wall

Elements installed to define rooms are designated as walls. Surfaces of platforms are not referred to as walls, but as faces.

Wall Top

In Late Classic work at Tikal, masons completed wall construction by plastering inside and out and across the top of the walls. Wall-top plaster is a reliable diagnostic of Late Classic construction at Tikal.

Introduction

Nine of the structures described in this volume, 5D-91 through 99, line the Plaza of the Seven Temples immediately W of the South Acropolis. They were surveyed within the Tikal Project Standing Architecture Survey, that is, with little or no excavation. The parts not obscured by debris and still in place were measured directly and are shown in solid line; hidden and fallen parts are depicted in broken line.

Confidence in broken-line depictions varies considerably. In some cases, fallen features could be accurately projected from surviving fragments; they are shown in broken line because they were not actually seen, but we have a good fix on where they were. In other cases, hidden features are inferred from debris profiles so that broken line may indicate uncertainty about location, size, or form. For example, roofcomb tops, shown in broken line, must be understood as mere guesses. Doorway locations are often evident in debris contours, but the precise dimension of the opening remains unknown and the doorway shown in broken line is an estimate, though its location may be reasonably certain.

The vegetation covering these structures actually impedes their further collapse, and only the roots may be holding masonry together when mortar has degenerated. Hence, recording was done without removal of vegetation, partially extant rooms were not cleared, and even small plants were left in place. In some cases, it was obvious that a minor dig would resolve the location of a corner or a detail of a stair and so some minor cuts were made. Where vaults had partially collapsed, the broken face could be cleaned to provide details of construction.

In recent years, Guatemalan archaeologists have returned to the Plaza of the Seven Temples and conducted more extensive investigations. Reports on their findings can be found in the publications of project director Oswaldo Gómez (2006, 2007, 2008, 2013:27–36).

Structure 5D-91

This structure is relatively well preserved, with intact vaulting, interior plaster, benches, cord holders, rope anchors, subspring beam sockets, doorway beam sockets, rod-row holes, vents, upper-zone sculpture, lintel beams, vault beams, roof structures with accessible interior spaces, and roof-structure sculpture. It occupies the center position at the S edge of the Plaza of the Seven Temples (Fig. 1). By ill luck, the S boundary of the 5D square passes right through 5D-91, so that only part of it appears on the Great Plaza sheet (TR. 11).

On the 1:6,250 sheet showing the whole of the mapped area (TR. 11), the position of 5D-91 can be better appreciated. It is one of the features forming the edge of epicentral Tikal in the SW quarter. To the S of 5D-91, there are only small structures widely separated. It seems likely that trees, bushes, and agricultural plots occupied these in-between areas S of 5D-91. To its N, 5D-91 is connected to all the other epicentral structures by continuous plaster paving. This position is particularly significant in that 5D-91 is a portal-type structure. It has such a magnitude and is so richly elaborated with sculptural detail that it could have served effectively as a major gateway into the epicenter from the SW.

Loten recorded Str. 5D-91 with Felipe Lanza as assistant and Walter Heinz as volunteer photographer during January 1966. Excavations were limited to a few probes through debris within the building, partial sectioning of the E bench, limited clearing in front of the W bench, and partial clearing at the W end of the central roof-structure unit. These operations produced no artifacts and no occupation debris.

Scaffolding was erected at the E end of the building to record sculptural details in the upper zone.

Both Maler (1911) and Tozzer (1911) mention Str. 5D-91. In the Tozzer/Merwin map, it is designated as number 60. Tozzer's fig. 39 illustrates the plan correctly, although his fig. 40 shows an incorrect section lacking the roof structures and with a solid wall wrongly positioned opposite a doorway opening.

Maler notes upper-zone masks "over every doorway" (1911:54). By 1966, none remained and debris that has accumulated against tree trunks (Fig. 2) on the substructure must have fallen relatively recently. Any such masks must have fallen since Maler's visit. His pl. 11 shows lintel failure and upper-zone collapse over the E doorway in the N facade (Dr. 5, Fig. 3). Clearly, upper-zone material above this doorway had already fallen. Therefore, "over every doorway" could not be entirely correct, but he may have seen masks over some doorways. He also noted some wall holes that suggested looter activity.

Construction Stages

Absence of formal pause-lines marked by plastered surfaces below wall-top level show that walls, building platform, and lower substructure platform were installed during the same construction stages. A rough mortar level sustains building walls, evidence that the building platform was not completely finished and plastered before wall construction began. Wall and building platform surfaces must have been plastered at the same time. The separation between building platform and lower substructure is similar. Hence, these three visually distinct features represent a single construction stage and they are substages within the same construction stage.

Lower Substructure Platform, Building Platform, and Building Walls

LOWER SUBSTRUCTURE PLATFORM

Debris, collapse, and vegetation, including many large trees, obscure details of the lower substructure (Fig. 2, 4, 5). Three terraces are assumed, but only because of the overall height of 7.6 m. Debris contours indicate very wide stairs extending across all three doorways on both N and S facades. Tread and riser details are inaccessible without excavation, so the reconstruction illustrated is merely conventional. Nevertheless, each of these two stairs must have required a masonry volume of nearly 2,000 m³. The three terraces amount to a masonry volume of 3,547 m³ as conjecturally reconstructed. The terraces are shown (in broken line) without apron moldings, but this is not meant to imply absence of such features, merely absence of data.

BUILDING PLATFORM

Debris laps above wall-foot level except for one small exposure at the E end (Fig. 2, 5, 6). Here, a building platform is indicated by masonry projecting beyond the wall face, though not to a finished edge. Neither extent of projection nor height can be determined without excavation. Projection of 0.25 m, height of 0.40 m, and near-vertical profile are all assumed. This yields a masonry volume estimate of 78 m³.

BUILDING WALLS

Primary walls, that is, exterior walls, are 2.9 m high by 1.45 m thick, a ratio of exactly 1:2 with little or no variation (Fig. 3–12). Corner angles vary from the true right angle by only a single degree (89°, 90°, 91°, and 90°). The 1° error results in E and W wall lengths of 4.95 and 4.83 m respectively. North and S wall lengths are identical (30.75 m). Thus, the error amounts to 0.12 m in 30.75 m or 0.039%. This small

departure from geometric precision escapes casual notice. Corners all appear square. Length of the building is 6.3 times average width.

The N wall at its exterior face bears 89° from N (magnetic). That is, 1° N of E (magnetic). Using the 1960 declination noted on TR. 11 map sheets, this equates to 5°, 45' S of true E.

The four outer corners are rounded with radii of 7, 10, 8, and 8 cm. At doorway openings, exterior corners are also rounded with radii of 6, 6, 7, 7, 10, 8, 8, and 10 cm. Interior corner rounding of the same doorways is comparable. This shaping of corners clearly was done after masonry had been installed. Corner rounding at doorways in secondary partitions is similar. If all wall corner rounding was meant to be identical, the variation tells us something about ancient Maya dimensional precision. Rounding may have been done by eye, so that all corners look similar. In other words, the workers probably used qualitative rather than quantitative criteria. This may apply rather generally and may be the reason why a consistent unit of measurement is not obvious.

Exterior wall faces in S and N facades are vertical. The exterior E end has a slight batter. The W end is vertical. Interior primary wall faces have slight negative batter. Secondary partitions have more pronounced negative batter on faces remote from the building centerline, while faces proximal to the centerline are vertical.

Hard, smooth, plastered wall-top surfaces are present only on primary walls. They step down an average of 0.25 m beside doorway openings for lintel beds. Primary vault springs and medial moldings are set at wall-top level.

Exterior wall-facing stones are block-type. Depths from face to butt exceed heights and even approach face lengths (Table 2.1).

The few depth measurements possible range from 0.20 to 0.30 m. Headers are probably present

TABLE 2.1
Structure 5D-91: Face Dimensions of Exterior Wall-Facing Stones

Dimension	n	Mean (m)	Standard Deviation	Range (m)
Face Length	100	28.84	8.75	0.19–0.57
Face Height	100	13.31	2.88	0.06–0.20

but cannot be identified by surface inspection. Joints are thin and spalls are few. It is evident that heights are more consistent than lengths, not surprising in that the stones are coursed, though not consistently, over the whole building. All facing stones have been dressed to a smooth wall face after masonry installation at the exterior, but interior surfaces are not similarly smoothed.

VENTS

Built into primary walls are 10 openings averaging about 0.15 m², set ca. 2.30 m above interior floor level (Fig. 3–7). They run horizontally through wall core and appear formed by masonry units. That is, they do not look like casts left by wood members such as scaffolding beams. The openings are spaced very regularly and opposite each other in both N and S walls as well as in E and W walls. All eventually were blocked at the interior by secondary construction, but one is now open where some of this material has fallen (Fig. 3 and 10). They are too small to have served as windows and, in any case, are set well above eye-level. They are designated as vents mainly because no other opening type seems appropriate.

An opening can be seen below one of the vent openings (Fig. 6:3). This is the only hole visible in exterior wall surfaces other than the vents discussed above. It may be a scaffolding hole. Debris above wall-foot level may conceal more such holes.

DOORWAYS

Three doorway openings occupy each of the N and S facades. Their alignment would facilitate through-circulation. For this reason, Str. 5D-91 may be regarded as a portal structure, though one that may well have served other activities, particularly as secondarily modified (see below).

Axial Dr. 1 and 4 (Fig. 3, 7) are 2.53 m wide, slightly greater than flanking Dr. 2, 3, 5, and 6 at 2.35 m. Thus, an emphasis on the axial position is present, but scarcely perceptible (Fig. 5). Concern for symmetry might call for recognition of the axis as a normal convention of architectural design. The extent to which this typifies Tikal architecture is taken up in TR. 34A. On the other hand, a portal structure might require a wider open-

ing on the central axis for purposes of ceremonial procession and/or celebrated entry. If this were really the issue, one might expect more of a difference between the axial and non-axial doorways.

JAMB SOCKETS

Sockets for removable doorway beams are visible in the jambs of four doorways (Fig. 3, 7). In three cases the holes probably represent upper members of vertically aligned pairs, the lower member hidden by debris. In each case socket depth in one jamb exceeds depth in the opposite jamb (Table 2.2). Depth differences would allow for removal of the rods.

Absence of sockets in Dr. 4 and 5 reflects debris coverage. Average diameter is 10 cm. The holes are not centered in jambs, but are offset toward N jamb edges. Wooden rods set into the sockets may have supported doorway closing devices, such as panels of vertical boards lashed to the rods. They lie near the interior for doorways in the S wall and the exterior for those in the N wall. Opening and closing may have been done from the Plaza side.

Doorway 6 (Fig. 3) is the exception, with two sets of socket holes at the upper level, the lower ones not accessible. In this case, a panel of vertical boards could have been set against one vertical pair and locked in place by the other. The locking pair could have been either exterior or interior.

All jamb sockets appear secondary, but this might not necessarily indicate installation after an initial period of use without doorway closers. Even if they were installed as primary features, such small pockets, ca. 10 cm in diameter, would not have been plastered in—they would have been cut into plas-

TABLE 2.2
Structure 5D-91: Doorway Closure Rods
(for rod numbers see Figure 3, 7, and 8)

Doorway	Rod	Left Socket Depth (m)	Right Socket Depth (m)	Diameter
1	3	0.10	0.23	?
2	4	0.10	0.24	0.07
3	5	0.10	0.06	?
6	1	0.10	0.16	?
	2	0.30	0.21	?

ter whether new or old. In either case, they seem rather cumbersome for everyday use and may indicate some kind of periodic function. If the primary function was indeed that of a grand entry into the Plaza, and perhaps into epicentral Tikal, doorways may have been closed for considerable periods between events. Vent holes may have been needed for the closed-up interludes. If they belong with other genuinely secondary features, in use at a time when occupancy of some sort seems indicated (see the discussion of secondary partitions below), their role seems less clear. Operating could have been done from within for nightly closing, though other less cumbersome devices are common at Tikal for this purpose. Hence, they may relate to primary function and indicate that the building was closed for extended periods and opened for specific events.

INTERIOR ROOM ARRANGEMENT

The single room defined by primary walls is 2 m wide and 27.8 m in length, a width-to-length ratio of 1:13.9. Room area (55.6 m²) amounts to 37% of gross building area (Fig. 4). Height from floor to vault cap is 4.73 m. Floor plaster abuts primary wall plaster and runs under the two benches at E and W ends of the room. It is hard, smooth, and white at the few exposed locations, but thickness and composition remain unknown. Evidence of burning on the floor surface and on the face of the secondary wall block appeared under the E bench.

SUBSPRING BEAMS

The former presence of subspring beams is inferred from pairing of holes opposite each other across the room (Table 2.3; Fig. 10, 11). Other holes

TABLE 2.3
Structure 5D-91: Subspring Beams

Beam Number	Socket Number	Height Below Wall	Diameter (m)	Depth (m)	Condition
1	14	?	0.08	0.22	Empty
1	49	1.0	0.09	0.11	Empty
2	15	?	0.07	0.04	Empty
2	48	?	?	0.02	Empty
3	16	?	0.04	0.10	Empty
3	47	?	0.04	0.10	Empty
4	23	?	0.07	0.07	Empty
4	43	0.10	0.07	0.07	Empty
5	28	?	0.08	?	Empty
5	37	1.0	0.08	0.08	Empty
6	29	?	0.08	?	Empty
6	?	?	?	?	?
7	26	?	?	?	Empty
7	40	0.58	0.08	?	Beam impression
8	19*	0.37	0.12	?	Beam intact
8					
9	28*	0.37	0.10	?	Empty
9	?	?	?	?	?

*See Fig. 5

lack an opposite number and are more enigmatic (see "Miscellaneous Wall Holes" below). The discussion of beams below, is entirely based on paired socket holes; none of the beams survived. Subspring beam locations are noted in Fig. 3 and 7.

Beams 1, 2, and 6 were installed in socket holes deeper at one end than at the other. These could easily be removed and reinstalled. The N socket of Bm. 6 is the only one retaining beam impressions in mortar, and this appears to be secondary to primary wall plaster. It may have been removable initially and later set permanently. Removal scars are not visible at any sockets, but may be obscured by the irregular shapes of the holes. Beams 3, 4, and 5 were set in sockets of equal depth and hence would not be removable. Beam 3 lies above the edge of the E bench and might have been installed with it; it could have held a curtain to close off the bench, which is low and might have been for sleeping. Beams 4 and 7 flank the center doorways, and might be primary installations holding curtains to isolate the axial passage through the building. Beams 1 and 2, above the E bench, might have supported a shelf. Beam 5 is adjacent to a secondary partition and may be contemporary with it. Beam 6 crosses the room just E of the W pair of doorways and as a screening device

it seems somewhat redundant. All subspring beams are set above the average height of the ancient Maya, so they could walk under them when closing devices such as curtains were pulled aside.

MISCELLANEOUS WALL HOLES

Six holes in primary walls cannot be assigned to beams (Fig. 3, 7, 10, 11). They are noted in Fig. 3 and 7. Two relatively large holes (2 and 5 on Fig. 10) are 0.22 and 0.26 m in diameter by 0.28 and 0.32 m deep; they may reflect looting efforts. On the exterior near the W end, holes 8 and 9 are 10 cm in diameter and 10 cm deep, and may have been made by a ladder accessing the roof (Table 2.4).

Lintels and Vaults

LINTELS

Once walls had been completed and plastered, the next step in construction began with installation of wood lintels over the six doorways (Table 2.5; Fig. 8, 10–13a). Lintel beams are of logwood unmodified except for slight smoothing on some tops and undersides. Butt ends are concealed behind masonry finished flush to the wall face at

TABLE 2.4
Structure 5D-91: Miscellaneous Wall Holes

Hole Number	Figure 10,11	Height* (m)	Diameter (m)	Depth (m)	Comment
1	4	?	0.15	0.81	Scaffolding hole?
2	12	1.65	0.22	0.28	Looter?
3	32	1.10	0.12	0.42	
4	38	1.28	0.14	0.02	
5	41	0.95	0.26	0.32	Looter?
6	42	0.58	0.08	0.10	
7	45	0.40	0.10	0.05	
8	50	?	0.10	0.10	Ladder anchor?
9	51	?	0.10	0.10	Ladder anchor?
10	6	1.10**	0.22	0.60	Scaffolding hole?

*Below vault spring
**Below superior molding

TABLE 2.5
Structure 5D-91: Lintel Beams

Door Number	No. of Beams	Diameter (avg. m)	Butt Length (m)	Total Length (m)	Surviving Members
1	10?	0.10	?	?	5 Beams, 3 Butts
2	10	?	0.60–0.70	3.50	8 Beams, 2 Butts
3	8	0.12–0.16	0.70	3.90	2 Beams
4	9	?	0.64–0.70	3.90	2 Beams
5	9? or 10?	?	?	?	1 Beam, 3 Butts
6	8	0.10–0.14	?	?	2 Butts, 6 Casts
7	19	0.08?		?	8 Beams
8	17	0.09?	?		6 Beams

both exterior and interior. The lintel beds are only 0.25 m below wall-top level and vault springs are at wall-top level. Hence, there is only about 0.10 m of supra-lintel masonry, little more than mortar and some aggregate.

The six primary lintels vary between nine and ten beams of unmodified logwood. Beam diameters vary as shown in Table 2.5. Scraps of plaster remaining in a few places imply that the wood surfaces were originally not exposed. Corresponding plaster-cover may have been omitted on lintels over secondary doorways, and these lintels employ almost twice as many beams. In one case, over Dr. 8, a larger diameter beam appears to have been flattened on both upper and lower surfaces (Table 2.6).

VAULT BEAMS

With lintels in place, workers installed 37 vault beams spanning the 2 half-vaults (Fig. 10, 11). They were set in place prior to vault masonry to control soffit profiles. Two observations support this view. First, the beams are not set at course levels. As a result, soffit stones had to be cut to fit around them at mid-course heights. The beams must have been in position before the masonry was installed. If the beams had been placed at the same time as the masonry, they likely would have been set at course levels. Second, the wall-top slopes upward 8 cm from E to W, but the capstones are dead level. To achieve this, independent leveling control must have been applied to the top of the half-vault units. Both con-

ditions could be satisfied if a timber falsework was assembled within the room. A series of masts along the centerline of the room would project up through the gap between half-vault units. Beams could be lashed to the mast, and at the top a series of long planks supporting a mud channel filled with water would provide the level control. Angled rods attached to the beams would stabilize them and at the same time indicate a rough soffit angle. The final profile would be cut after the whole vault mass had been built up.

VAULTING

Three facets or steps divide the soffit into horizontal levels that extend across end-vault units as well as the long half-vaults (Fig. 8, 10–12). Workers cut the convex stepped profile into the soffit stones after they had been set in place. This is indicated by outsets that do not correspond to course levels. Each higher facet is more steeply pitched, so that the soffit is both stepped and convex.

Five unmodified logwood beams survive essentially intact and ten butts remain in their sockets. Nominal diameters range from 0.06 to 0.11 m. Socket depths, accessible in 26 cases, range from 0.26 to 1.03 m. Sockets open for inspection are straight and horizontal.

A coat of thin, white, hard plaster covers soffit surfaces hiding most of the masonry. Only a few vault stones are visible at points of collapse near and above doorway openings. Soffit-facing stones

TABLE 2.6
Structure 5D-91: Vault Beams

Room Number	Level	Diameter (m)	Depth* (m) S end	Depth* (m) N end	Condition
1	Low	0.06	0.67	0.60	Butt in S socket
2	Mid	0.10	0.26	?	Sockets empty
3	High	0.08	0.36	0.48	Intact
4	Low	0.11	?	?	Intact
5	Mid	0.09	?	0.34	Intact
6	High	0.08	0.60	0.96	Sockets empty
7	Low	0.09	?	?	Intact
8	Mid	0.10	0.61	0.58	2 butts
9	High	0.08	0.47	0.35	Intact
10	Low	0.11	0.45	0.57	2 butts
11	Mid	0.10	1.03	0.88	Sockets empty
12	Low	0.08	?	?	Beam impressions**
13	High	?	?	?	In secondary partition?
14	Mid	0.08	0.82	0.64	Sockets empty
15	Low	0.08	0.53	0.53	Butt in S socket
16	High	0.08	0.57	0.65	Butt in S socket
17	Mid	0.08	0.52	0.49	2 butts
18	Low	?	?	?	Vault masonry fallen
19	High	0.08	0.42	0.47	Butt in S socket
20	Mid	0.10	?	?	Intact
21	Low	0.08	?	?	Sockets empty
22	High	0.08	0.90	0.70	Sockets empty
23	Mid	0.08	0.60	0.42	Sockets empty
24	High	0.10	0.79	0.53	Sockets empty
25	Low	0.09	0.50	0.68	Sockets empty
26	Low	?	0.60	0.50	Removed?
27	High	0.09	?	0.50	Intact
28	Low	0.09	?	?	Sockets empty
29	Mid	0.09	0.68	?	Intact
30	High	0.08	0.67	0.70	Intact
31	Mid	0.09	?	?	Intact
32	Low	0.10	?	?	Intact
33	Mid	0.10	?	?	Sockets empty
34	High	0.10	?	?	Sockets empty
35	High	0.09	?	?	Sockets empty
36	Low	?	?	?	Assumed in secondary wall

*Socket depth
**May have been carved

TABLE 2.7
Structure 5D-91: Vault-Soffit Facing-Stone Dimensions

Dimension	n	Mean (m)	Standard Deviation	Range (m)
Face Height	21	0.29	9.81	0.24–0.36
Face Length	21	0.26	2.49	0.20–0.30
Depth	14	0.66	6.37	0.54–0.75

are almost square on the face with the greater dimension vertical (Table 2.7). Coursing is regular and continuous, and each soffit is six courses high (Table 2.7).

The high value of standard deviation for height (9.81) partly reflects the small size of the sample. But even so, this is a surprising value in coursed masonry. Lengths are usually more variable than heights. The implication is that course heights vary more than individual stones within courses. By extension it may be inferred that masonry units were prepared course by course.

After face dressing of soffit surfaces, a thin coat of hard white plaster completed the half-vault stage of construction. Soffit plaster turns out onto the top surface of the uppermost course of masonry. That is, capstones were installed after soffits had been plastered.

Upper-zone collapse has exposed vault-back surface in several places, generally above doorways. The vault-back is an undulating coat of hard plaster that turns out onto the top surface of medial moldings (Fig. 8, 12). At the top of the vault, it merges with soffit plaster. That is, it was installed prior to vault caps.

Medial molding stones form the lower border of the upper zone, but were set in place together with vault construction. They are the largest masonry units in visible parts of the structure. A representative length is 0.40 m; height is 0.35 m and depth is 0.70 m. The stones are sharply tapered from face to butt.

Rod Row

As workers installed medial molding stones they also set in place a series of wooden members (Fig. 6:1, 8:3). The evidence for these units is a series of

holes designated in Tikal Project terminology as a "rod row." They are casts in the mortar between the stones left by tapered wooden dowels ranging from 3 to 7 cm in diameter at the wall surface. The casts indicate that the wood dowels were carefully shaped to a circular cross section. They are spaced somewhat irregularly from 0.58 to 1.48 m apart across both N and S facades in the angle where the underside of the medial molding meets the wall face (Fig. 6:1, 8:3). They slant upward into the mortar at angles ranging from 5° to 50°. Variations in spacing reflect varying dimensions of medial molding stones; two medial molding stones intervene between each rod-row hole. The dowels presumably projected some way out from the wall face. They could have been used to suspend tapestries or fabrics of some kind. Apparently, they passed over the doorways and across the ends, hiding walls and doorways.

With vaults completed, workers would have dismantled the timber falsework—leaving vault beams now anchored in masonry—and installed preplastered capstones to close the gap between half-vault units. The capstones are flat slabs, regular in dimensions, and plastered prior to installation over the (badly eroded) central part exposed within the room.

Upper Zone and Roof

The next operation, following on vault completion, is the upper zone and roof (Fig. 2, 5, 8, 12, 13b, 14a,b, 18a,b). Core masonry of medium-to-large rubble aggregate abuts the smooth vault-back plaster and covers the capstones to a depth of 0.20–0.30 m. On this is a topping of 4 cm of small aggregate in tight gray mortar finished with hard smooth plaster. Where protected by the roof structure, roof plaster showed no signs of weathering. Surviving surface at roof center is level, but may have sloped down slightly to the superior molding (this part eroded away).

Upper-zone core masonry builds out to provide backing for the carved upper-zone facing stones. Uncarved facing stones are thin slabs, of veneer type, set on edge. Only a few remained. Representative dimensions are 0.60 m in length, 0.32 m in height, and 0.09 m in thickness (depth). Upper-zone batter is slight on N and S facades and even less on the short E and W ends. Superior molding stones survived in two places. They are very similar to medial molding units.

Sculptural features occupy the four corners (Fig. 18a,b, 19a,b). Realistic human faces gaze outward diagonally. Complex headdress elements surround them, terminated by vertical stacks of knotted plumes. Sculptural work is carved in stone and covered with thin plaster. Some details are modeled in stucco and the only trace of color is one small patch of red on the medial molding. The four corner motifs appear essentially the same, although there are some variations in detail.

Away from the corners, most upper-zone sculpture has been lost. Two areas on the N facade retain fragments that appear to be outer edges of sculptural features centered on the two flanking doorways (Fig. 5, 13b, 16b). Sculptural treatment probably filled both N and S upper zones. The short facades at E and W are occupied by the headdress details of the corner masks.

ROOF-STRUCTURE UNITS

Absence of weathering on roof plaster under roof-structure features indicates that they are part of primary construction (Fig. 2, 5, 8, 9, 15, 16a,b, 21a). They could well have been underway while upper-zone finishing was still in progress, since this finishing operation would have been protracted and time-consuming. In character, they lie somewhere between roofcombs and upper stories. Five vaulted rooms connected by arched screens are accessible through low vaulted doorways. The central room offered a greater amount of surviving detail and is the only one examined internally. It has four windows, paired opposite each other in the N and S facades. At each end are vaulted doorway openings 0.77 m high by 0.47 m wide. Jamb stones forming the upper 0.25 m are cut on an angle to form a vault one course high. They leave a gap of 0.20 m capped

by a flat stone. Entry through these doorways is by crawling. There is no sign of a closing device, but a low sill would deter rainwater. The others, less well preserved, appear similar except that the end units have only one doorway.

Immediately inside the doorways at each end, a vaulted element forms a kind of vestibule. Its spring is set 1.3 m above floor (roof) level and projects 0.10 m from the inner wall face. For want of an established term it is designated as a "shoulder vault." It "shoulders" out from the larger vault surface (Fig. 8). Soffit stones are all headers of representative size, 0.18 m in length and 0.30 m in height, not face-dressed after installation.

Between these "vestibule" vaults, room space expands to form a central volume enclosed by inwardly inclined walls. The effect is that of vaults springing from floor level and without vault beams. Original height is lost due to collapse. Reconstructed height is 2.5 m, leaving the cap to span 0.45 m, which is rather wide. The original height might have been greater, but if so the volume of collapse debris would be greater.

Facing stones within these central spaces are all stretchers ranging in length from 0.40 to 0.60 m and in height from 0.30 to 0.34 m, not face-dressed after installation. The floor is a thin plaster coat, 1 cm thick, on top of the roof plaster and abutting wall plaster. Just inside the doorway a second very thin floor is visible; it turns up to walls and to the doorway sill.

Externally, corresponding to the central interior space, large sculptural features elaborate both N and S facades (Fig. 16a). The central element is a large, realistic human face, similar to those at the upper-zone corners. Only lower elements survive. Sculptural features appear similar in both facades, but there is not enough left to show whether they are completely identical.

Screens connecting the five roof features are reconstructed from stones found in debris on the roof and in situ at the W doorway to the central unit (Fig. 5, 8, 10–12). The arches they form have straight-line soffit profiles.

Secondary Modifications

After a period of use as originally formed, the building underwent a series of modifications that may indicate a substantial change in function. The original room is divided by two partitions that appear clearly secondary (Fig. 10, 11), that is, they abut primary wall and vault plaster, engulf several vault beams, and block up all the vents in primary walls. Secondary wall and vault units form E and W ends of the rooms defined by the partitions. These units seem to have no obvious purpose other than making the new rooms smaller. They appear related to the partitions, but at the W end some of this material has either fallen or been pulled down exposing primary end-vault surface with no plaster. The plaster may have been removed for a better bond with primary fabric. This circumstance, however, throws the status of the end units into question—they probably are secondary, installed with the partitions, but this remains uncertain.

Secondary partitions (Fig. 17a) are 1.8 m thick, more massive than needed for non-load-bearing members. After installation, with drying of the mortar, their upper parts shrank away from primary vault plaster leaving a gap of about 1 cm. This demonstrates conclusively that the partitions never did carry any load other than their own weight. The builders may have meant to provide additional support or perhaps they wanted the new partitions to look like original features.

At the E end of the newly defined central room, a small excavation encountered a secondary floor 0.15 m in thickness. Presumably this extends through the new central room, the internal doorways, and the outer doorways. There would then have been a step up from the lateral rooms into the central room. The step from the exterior lower substructure into the central room would have been increased to 0.60 m.

ROPE ANCHOR

The W face of the E partition presents a feature that is designated here as a "rope anchor" (Fig. 10, 13a, 20a). In effect, it is a very large cord holder with the bar set horizontally just below wall-top level. The bar may be a subspring beam set in primary walls and later incorporated into the secondary partition with only its middle part exposed in a square recess. There should have been a corresponding anchor in the E face of the W partition, but this material has either collapsed or been pulled down.

The surviving rope anchor is stout enough to serve for something quite heavy. Presumably some

device stretched between the anchors down the length of the room on its centerline. The setup looks excellent for a hammock slung between the two N and S doorways to take advantage of any breeze and the shade offered by the building. Perhaps more plausibly, a tapestry or fabric could have been hung from it, blocking the path of through-circulation on the central axis.

Blocking up of the wall vents suggests that primary doorways remained open. This too suggests a radical change in function. Maler (1911:53) described the structure as a "palace," that is, residential; he may have been right with respect to the modified structure. His photograph (pl. 10) shows that collapse of the W rope anchor had taken place earlier than his visit.

Lintel beams 0.06 to 0.16 m in diameter span the doorways in the partitions. Their butts extend the full width of the room. As a result, upper-partition masonry, mimicking primary vault facets, rests on a layer of timber. Deterioration of the beams may have induced partial collapse of this pseudo-vault material.

CORD HOLDERS

Just below the rope anchor, two cord holders flank the doorway in the partition (Fig. 13a). They have unplastered circular recesses and once contained vertical wood pegs now rotted away. Other cord holders may remain hidden by debris.

SEALED DOORWAYS

Plastered screens sealed doorways in secondary partitions (Fig. 3, 4, 7). The W doorway jambs retain beam holes and plaster-turns as evidence for this closure. The E doorway has only one vertical, very faint plaster-turn. The seals probably involved wattle and daub frames coated with plaster on both sides. Remnants are so scrappy that simple deterioration seems unlikely, and they may have been removed deliberately.

BENCHES

Benches abut secondary wall units at E and W ends of the building (Fig. 3, 4, 7, 20b). The W bench (Fig. 20b) is very well made, finished with hard smooth plaster and has an upright at the back. It resembles a throne. The E bench is low and of much rougher construction. It might have been for sleeping. A small excavation at the E end exposed a floor that had been heavily burned, and burn marks extended up the secondary wall face.

GRAFFITI

Graffiti abound on both primary and secondary wall surfaces (TR. 31:fig. 6a, 15). One motif, on the N jamb of the W secondary doorjamb, has stratigraphic control. It is a crudely pecked inverted "U" containing an element that resembles a phallus. Plaster-turns that run over this graffito show it was already present when the doorway was sealed up. Therefore, this particular graffito was inscribed during the second time span of building use.

Relationship to Adjacent Stratigraphy

No stratigraphic data are available. Similarity in architectural attributes suggests that the two structures closely adjacent to it, 5D-90 and 5D-92, are contemporary.

Architecture

Structure 5D-91 combines "temple" and "range-type" attributes. The building is long and narrow, in the "range-type" category, though the substructure is quite high and the roof structures resemble roof-combs in form, but contain accessible rooms like a second story.

Because of the large stairs on N and S facades, and the arrangement of doorways opposite each other for passage, 5D-91 may be classed as a "portal structure." As initially built, entry into and exit out of the Plaza of the Seven Temples probably constituted its primary function. Obviously, such an elaborate installation would not have been needed simply for entering and exiting the Plaza. Structure 5D-91 strongly formalized these movements and probably also provided for some access control. Screening or purification may have taken place within the building. Secondary modifications subdivided the original single room into three rooms. This change still allowed for passage, but may have been made either to accommodate other activities or to enhance the original ones. As a purely speculative example, some persons may have been able to enter or leave without much ceremony, while others might have required greater treatment. Secondarily defined off-axial room spaces could have served the more protracted processes.

Lateral and front-to-rear symmetry characterize the format. Nothing extant distinguishes front from rear. Since the structure faces N onto a well-defined Plaza, this facade might be regarded as the "front." On the other hand, people of ancient Tikal approaching the epicentral complex of monumental structures from the S might well have seen the S facade as the "front." The central doorway, wider than the others, marks a N-S axial line of symmetry. Only the two very different interior benches violate this balance.

Summarizing TR. 34A findings, some attributes of 5D-91 suggest a late date of construction. These include floor turn up to wall plaster; wall tops plastered; lintel bed plastered; preplastered capstones; plastered vault-backs (Fig. 17b); post-dressing of interior and exterior wall masonry; upper-zone sculpture carved in stone; specialized vault stones; and room area only one-third of gross building area.

Within the time frame of late construction, some attributes imply an early position. These include relatively small wall-facing stones of block type; lack of or weak distinction between headers and stretchers in wall facing; irregular coursing of wall facing; upper zone relatively low in relation to wall height; and a high ratio value of room length against room width.

Symmetrical arrangement and similarity of debris profiles imply that 5D-91 is the central feature of a triadic composition completed by flanking structures 5D-90 and 92. Both have collapsed more completely than 5D-91, but 5D-92 retains enough accessible features for a separate report (see Str. 5D-92 this volume). This triadic grouping compares with the seven structures along the E edge of the Plaza (5D-93 through 99), and the set of four forming its N edge (5D-78 through 81). Groups or sets of structures, seem to have been a theme developed around this Plaza. By contrast, its W side is defined by rear facades of structures facing into the Plaza dominated by Str. 5C-54, the Lost World Pyramid (Table 2.8).

TABLE 2.8
Structure 5D-91: Time Spans

Time Span	Floor	Comment
1		Period of final abandonment. Collapse of some upper-zone material relatively recently. No evidence of occupation.
2		Period of use as modified by addition of E bench. This feature may indicate occupation.
3	Fl. 2 (in roof structure)	Period of use as modified by insertion of secondary partitions in the building and renewal of floor surface in the roof structure.
4	Fl. 1 (in building)	Period of primary construction (6,115 m^3) and use as initially intended. Closing devices in exterior doorways? No evidence of occupancy.

III

Structure 5D-92

The SE corner of the Plaza of the Seven Temples is effectively closed off by the debris of Str. 5D-92 (Fig. 1). A narrow opening to the E probably existed between this structure and 5D-93 (Fig. 22a,b). Debris from both structures now obscures any passage that may have once been open. In 5D-92, all vaults have at least partially fallen and the interior is choked with debris (Fig. 22b). Nevertheless, enough accessible fabric remained to permit inclusion in the architectural survey.

Loten recorded 5D-92 in 1966 with Felipe Lanza as assistant. Clearing was kept to a minimum, in line with the terms of the architectural survey. Very limited excavations were made at the N axial doorway, on the stair (Fig. 23a), and at the central roof-structure unit.

Maler described 5D-92 as having "three doorways on the north" (1911:53). In 1966, the N facade was entirely fallen and the presence of seven doorways appears more likely than three (there would have been more wall debris if there had only been three doorways). Maler reported that the upper zone (frieze) "was quite plain." The small portion of upper-zone material in situ at the E end (Fig. 24a,b) is now too weathered to determine, though preservation must have been better in his day. Maler gives the building length as 20.34 m. Tozzer provides a plan (1911:fig. 38), also assuming three doorways in the N facade. His length is 66.4 feet (20.24 m). The length currently measured for the building component is 19.5 m.

Construction Stages

Presumably work on construction stages would have begun with preparation of the foundation. Whether this engaged earlier construction is not known. No sustaining surface was accessible without undue excavation.

Substructure, Lower Substructure Platform, and Building Platform

SUBSTRUCTURE

Due to debris cover, the nature of the substructure is not fully known. Two components, building platform and lower substructure platform, comprise the substructure. Both are part of one construction stage (Fig. 23b).

LOWER SUBSTRUCTURE PLATFORM

The lower substructure platform is the part of the structure completely concealed beneath debris. Its form, as illustrated (Fig. 25, 26), is conjectural. Two terraces are assumed on grounds that a single terrace would be unusually high. No moldings are shown, but apron profiles may exist.

A good, hard plaster surface that appears to be the top of the lower substructure platform turns up to the building platform (Fig. 23b). Clearly, building platform masonry had been installed prior to completion of the lower substructure platform. This demonstrates that both components were indeed assembled during the same stage of construction.

Debris profiles indicate the presence of a very broad stair on the N side. A very small excavation exposed a tread and riser (0.32 and 0.26 m) near the middle of the stair (Fig. 23a). The stair shown is reconstructed on this basis. Absence of stair-side ramps (balustrades, or *alfardas*) is assumed. The two partial risers actually seen appear to be vertical, made up of several courses of relatively small masonry units.

On the S facade, vault elements protrude through the debris surface (Fig. 26). These reveal the presence of a room or rooms at lower substructure level. No details are available without more excavation than would be appropriate in the architectural survey.

Collapse patterns imply presence of at least one doorway. Any room(s) here would have been accessible from the S, that is, from outside the epicentral complex of structures connected by continuous plaster pavement. If entry to epicentral Tikal was part of the function of the structures along the S edge of the Plaza of the Seven Temples, rooms that opened to the exterior may have been for personnel controlling such entry.

There is also, of course, the possibility that these vault elements belong to an earlier structure and were not originally part of the 5D-92 substructure. Extensive excavation would be needed to verify this.

BUILDING PLATFORM

As seen 1 m W of the centerline (Fig. 23b), the building platform is 0.46 m high, vertical, and built up in three courses. It projects 5 cm from the wall face. The surface running under it is an uneven layer of small stones, suggesting a floor-preparation surface. This is probably material of the lower substructure platform. No building platform plaster survived at the one accessible location. A single building platform level is assumed throughout the structure, although there is a slight variation in vault-spring levels from N to S (Fig. 23b).

Building

The exterior configuration, or "footprint" of the building, is a simple rectangle 19.5 m long by 6.96 m wide (width:length ratio is 1:2.8)(Fig. 25). There are no insets, outsets, or other articulations of the geometry. The only corner measurable is less than 1° from a right angle (89°, 15' magnetic). Orientation is best measured along the E-W walls since N-S walls are short and less well preserved. The azimuth of the N side of the central spine wall is 89.3°, less than 1° N of E magnetic.

BUILDING WALLS

As seen at one location (Fig. 28), a hard plaster surface runs under the walls of the building. This appears to be the top surface of the building platform applied on completion of the substructure. The tops of the walls are sealed by hard, smooth, wall-top plaster. All wall faces examined are vertical. Clearly the walls of the building were installed as one distinct construction stage.

The axial lintel bed—the only one extant—is finished with much rougher plaster, apparently

TABLE 3.1
Structure 5D-92: Wall-Facing Masonry Dimensions

Dimension	n	Mean (m)	Standard Deviation	Variance	Range (m)
Ext. Length	100	0.30	9.8	95.8	0.13–0.67
Ext. Height	100	0.14	4.9		0.06–0.32
Int. Length	30	0.35	8.3		0.22–0.60
Int. Height	30	0.18	5.1		0.07–0.28

continuous with the wall top but not hardened (probably by pounding) or smoothed (by rubbing). Apart from the slight difference noted above, wall tops maintain a constant level throughout the building.

Interior and exterior wall faces present very similar masonry attributes. Facing stones are of block type, horizontally bedded, rectangular, and inconsistently coursed (Table 3.1).

High values of standard deviation indicate weak dimensional control, particularly in face lengths. Mortar joints are thin and spalls infrequent. Wall cores employ rubble masonry, which is not bedded. Interior and exterior faces present a smooth finish that was achieved by shaving or rubbing the stones after they had been set in the wall. This surface then received a single coat of hard, unpainted white plaster.

At one interior location where plaster had exfoliated, a reused facing stone was seen with plaster on its top surface (Fig. 29). Such a stone could have come from anywhere, but its presence may lead one to suspect an earlier structure on the same site, perhaps partially demolished. Vaults at substructure level may hint at the same thing.

Walls of the building enclose four rooms, one long room facing N (Fig. 29–32), and three shorter rooms facing S (Fig. 25, 28, 33, 34). Total room area is 52.8 m²; the relationship of room area to gross building area is 1:2.6 (Table 3.2).

The seven doorways of the N room employ the width of the spine-wall doorway as a standard dimension. Shallow debris profiles imply presence of multiple doorways across the N facade. Three axial doorways provide for through N-S circulation, but the S doorway leads only to a platform extension over the substructure rooms and does not allow for direct exit or entry to or from the Plaza of the Seven Temples.

Above debris in Rm. 1, four wall holes are visible, three in the W half of the room and one just E of the axial doorway (Fig. 29, 31). Diameters average 0.08 m and depths range from 0.08 to 0.20 m; they are cut into the plaster but could well be primary. Functional interpretation is hampered by loss of the opposite wall and concealment of any other holes that might exist beneath debris.

Rooms 2 and 4 provide additional subspring wall holes (Fig. 28, 34). Most are empty, but two (Fig. 28:2) have been plugged and sealed with plaster. Also in Rm. 2, three holes appear immediately under the vault spring, higher than usual for such features.

Three holes pass right through end walls from interior to exterior. Two appear in Rm. 2 (Fig. 28:1). They are vertically aligned and look like very good candidates for scaffolding holes. The hole in Rm. 4, corresponding to the upper hole in Rm. 2, has been crudely plugged with a stone that bulges out from the plaster face (Fig. 34:2). One would expect scaffolding holes to be plugged after construction, but not so roughly.

The W jamb surface of the axial doorway in the spine wall displays four holes, two empty and two plugged and sealed with plaster (Fig. 27a:5, 8). The space between this latter pair seems appropriate for a closure device of vertical boards. The two open holes seem too far apart for this and remain problematic. Additional holes vertically below these visible ones might appear on removal of debris.

Vaulting

The work undertaken as this stage of construction includes vault beams installed as part of a timber falsework, wood lintels over doorways, masonry of vault units, and medial molding stones. Completion of vaulting is marked by vault-back stucco turning down onto the tops of medial molding stones. Vault masonry survives over the central spine wall and the ends of rooms, but has fallen at outer walls at doorway locations. Vault height is 1.65 m and relates to wall height as 1:1.6.

TABLE 3.2
Structure 5D-92: Room Proportions

Room	Width:Length Ratio
1	1:10.9
2	1:3
3	1:3.8
4	1.3:1

TIMBER FALSEWORK

Evidence for a system of timber falsework can be seen in the setting levels of vault beams, which fall between course levels of the vault soffit. Masonry units of the soffit facing had to be cut to fit around the beams. This stands as proof that the beams were set in place prior to assembly of the masonry. The form of the falsework is conjectural, but might have involved a series of vertical poles running down the center of the room secured to scaffolding beams extending through the walls. Vault beams could then be lashed to the poles at desired levels, and diagonal poles or thin rods could be attached to the beams to set the soffit angles. Masons would be able to use these rods to guide the amount of overhang at each course level. After vault masonry had been built up to the full height, soffit faces could be finished by shaving and rubbing to a smooth profile. The plaster finish would then be applied. During this work, an open gap would be maintained at the top between vault units, and vertical poles of the falsework would extend up through this gap.

WOOD LINTELS

Only one lintel survives (Fig. 27a) with ten extant beams, one remaining butt, and one missing beam. Remaining beams are logwood, not modified in shape, perhaps installed complete with bark. Diameters range from 0.08 to 0.14 m and butts extend

0.50 m on bed surfaces. The lintel bed appears to be unusually irregular, about 0.10 m higher at the S side than at the N. There is no clear break between supra-lintel masonry and vault masonry.

VAULT MASONRY

Surviving soffits are five courses high. Coursing runs consistently over the E-W length of the double vault unit above the spine wall (Fig. 27a). Soffit stones are rectangular on the face and sharply tapered to toothed butts. Facings in both half-vault and end-vault units are all headers (Table 3.3).

Soffit facers are more standardized than wall facers, both in dimension and in shape. Mortar is thin at the surface, but thicker at the butt both in joints and in beds. Bedding surfaces slope sharply upward and spalls are absent. Surfaces were dressed to a smooth profile after installation of masonry and finished with a single coat of hard, white plaster, apparently unpainted. Spring levels rise approximately 0.10 m from the N room to the S rooms.

VAULT BEAMS

Empty sockets show that beams had been arranged in three levels (Fig. 28, 29, 31, 32, 34). Diameters range from 0.07 to 0.13 m and socket depths range from 0.25 to 0.73 m. Beam impressions in mortar imply that these members were unmodified poles, probably logwood. These values

TABLE 3.3
Structure 5D-92: Face Dimensions of Vault-Soffit Facing Stones

Dimension	n	Mean (m)	Standard Deviation	Range (m)
Length*	40	0.26	2.97	0.18–0.32
Height*	40	0.29	3.43	0.32–0.40
Length**	38	0.26	3.50	0.19–0.34
Height**	38	0.30	4.09	0.21–0.42
Depth***	9	0.56	6.25	0.50–0.64

*face length (height) in half-vault units
**face length (height) in end-vault units
***face-to-butt

TABLE 3.4
Structure 5D-92: Vault-Beam Sockets

Room Number	Beam Number	Diameter (m)	Depth (m)	Level
1	1	?	0.61	Low
1	2	0.08	0.50	High
1	3	?	0.36	Mid
1	4	0.10	0.47	Low
1	5	0.10	0.47	High
1	6	0.10	0.43	Mid
1	7	?	?	Low (bees' nest)
1	8	?	0.73	High
1	9	0.07	0.45	Mid
1	10	?	?	Low
1	11	0.12	?	High
1	12	0.12	0.49	Mid
1	13	0.07	0.50	Low
1	14	?	?	High (not extant)
1	15	0.09	0.32	Mid
1	16	0.07	0.69	Low
1	17	0.13	?	High (debris filled)
1	18	0.08	0.58	Mid
1	19	0.14	0.70	Low
1	20	0.08	0.40	Mid
1	21	0.12	0.55	Low
1	22	0.10	0.64	High
1	23	0.10	0.40	Mid
1	24	0.09	0.58	Low
1	25	0.07	?	High
1	26	0.10	0.43	Mid
1	27	0.10	0.30	Low
1	28	0.08	0.49	High
1	29	0.13	0.25	Mid
1	30	0.10	0.70	Low
2	1	0.06	?	Low
2	2	0.09	?	Mid
2	3	0.10	?	Low
2	4	0.09	?	High
2	5	0.10	?	Low
2	6	0.09	?	Mid
2	7	0.09	?	Low
2	8	?	?	High

TABLE 3.4 (cont'd)
Structure 5D-92: Vault-Beam Sockets

Room Number	Beam Number	Diameter (m)	Depth (m)	Level
2	9	0.08	?	Mid
2	10	0.12	?	Low
3	1	0.08	?	Low
3	2	0.09	?	High
3	3	0.11	?	Mid
3	4	0.08	?	Low
3	5	0.09	?	High
3	6	0.09	?	Mid
3	7	0.12	?	Low
3	8	0.13	?	High
4	1	0.09	?	Mid
4	2	0.10	?	Low
4	3	0.12	?	High
4	4	0.12	?	Mid
4	5	0.13	?	Low
4	6	0.10	?	High
4	7	0.10	?	Mid

are presented in Table 3.4. Mean values for depth are 0.57 m for low beams; 0.41 m for mid-height beams; and 0.54 m for high beams. Diameters vary only slightly around 0.10 m.

Roof and Upper Zones

Workers probably began this stage of construction by installing core masonry on top of medial molding stones. This material would have been built up to the level of the tops of the vault units. At this point, preplastered capstones would have been placed over the gap left between half-vault units after timber falsework had been removed, vault soffits had been plastered, and vault-back surfaces had been sealed with stucco.

Capstones are standardized rectangular blocks averaging 0.20 m in thickness. Widths range from 0.30 to 0.43 m (mean value is 0.37 m and standard deviation is 3.16, n=18). Undersurfaces are smoothly dressed and plastered over the exposed central part between half-vaults. Upper-zone facing masonry would have been placed in conjunction with backing material. A superior molding is assumed, but is not evident in accessible features.

A hard, smooth plastered surface roughly 0.20 m above the capstones (Fig. 27a:2) is almost certainly the roof. It survives only at the center under material of the roof structure. A distinct slope dropping from S to N is evident in the fragment that remains.

ROOF STRUCTURE

Masonry above roof level reveals the presence of a roof structure (Fig. 27a) that appears to run along the center of the roof in a series of separate units. Tree growth has greatly damaged and obscured this feature.

A small patch of plastered flooring seen slightly E of the axial line may be an interior floor (Fig. 27a:1). If so, then the original height must have been on the order of 2 m (maximum surviving height is roughly 1 m). An interior floor may indicate that the interior space of the roof structure was accessible.

Secondary Modifications

At the E end of Rm. 2, two floor surfaces are visible (Fig. 28:3), and it is assumed that the upper surface is secondary. Also in the E end of Rm. 2, two wall holes have been plugged and sealed with good plaster (Fig. 28:2). Two jamb holes are similarly plugged and sealed in the axial doorway passing through the spine wall.

Relationship to Adjacent Stratigraphy

The similar debris profiles of 5D-92 and 5D-90, the latter much more deteriorated, suggest that the two structures may form an identical pair. Their symmetry around 5D-91 further hints that all three structures may be elements of one architectural project.

Architecture

Two attributes classify 5D-92 as a "range-type" structure. These are horizontally extensive interior space and relatively low substructure (the height is approximately 3 m). Features that place it in a subcategory include vaulted rooms at lower-substructure level and a roof structure that may include accessible interior space.

The stair on the N shows that this facade was the "front." From the room arrangement and debris profiles, it seems clear that the S facade had fewer doorways, three assumed in the S and seven in the N.

Several attributes suggest a Late Classic date of construction. These include wall-top plaster, preplastered capstones, specialized vault stones, dressing of facing masonry after installation, and vault heights similar to wall heights.

Other attributes imply an early position within the Late Classic. These include the plastered top of the building platform that runs under the walls of the building, absence of consistent coursing in wall facings, and block-type wall facing stones of relatively small dimension (Table 3.5).

TABLE 3.5
Structure 5D-92: Time Spans

Time Span	Unit and Floor	Comment
1		Period of abandonment and collapse.
2	Floor	Period of use as modified by addition of Fl. 2 and by sealing of several wall holes.
3	Fl. 1	Period of functioning as originally built, probably in early years of the Late Classic period. Masonry volume ca. 1,740 m³.

IV

Structure 5D-93

Seven structures line the E side of the Plaza of the Seven Temples in the SW quadrant of epicentral Tikal. Symmetry and similarity suggest that all seven may represent a single architectural project. Activities connected with numerology of the number seven might have been located here. As Thompson pointed out years ago, the number seven is related to the jaguar and the night sun (Thompson 1950:134). These are very prominent aspects of ancient Maya belief, entirely appropriate for a major architectural installation.

Structure 5D-93 occupies the S end of the group (Fig. 1). Like the other six it faces toward the W, its front parts fallen and buried in debris. Cardinal orientation, based on rear walls, falls 7.5° W of magnetic N. That is, a perpendicular representing the cardinal orientation of the building lies 45' W of true N as measured for the Tikal Project base maps (TR. 11).

Recording was done in 1964 and 1965 by A.M. Nagy and in 1968 by M. Orrego. The Tozzer/Merwin map (Tozzer 1911) numbers the series as Str. 52–58. Maler's description concentrates on the central member, 5D-96 (Maler 1911:52). Tozzer noted a roofcomb chamber in Str. 5D-93 (Tozzer 1911:142). Collapse, subsequent to his visit, has obscured this feature.

Construction Stages

Although external architectural form suggests four components: lower substructure platform, building platform, building, and roofcomb, the joints between them are not formalized, that is, not finished with plaster. It seems evident that construction proceeded from base to top in a single operation. Lower parts were not necessarily completed before work had begun on parts higher up. In effect, then, there is only one construction stage. The various visually apparent "parts" are discussed below as substages.

Lower Substructure Platform, Building Platform, and Building Walls

LOWER SUBSTRUCTURE PLATFORM

Entirely obscured by debris, most attributes of this component can only be surmised (Fig. 35–39). A horizontal layer in exposed core masonry at the rear axial outset probably indicates the top surface. It is little more than a mortar bed but does extend across the core mass. Its height above Plaza level is 3.5 m.

The extent that the lower platform projects beyond the building platform is unclear. At the rear (Fig. 36), a modest projection seems indicated by the amount of accumulated debris. The same projection has been assumed for the sides and front (Fig. 37, 38). Apron profiles are assumed on the basis of their presence in the building platform, but their details are mere estimates. Terrace surfaces probably have batter, as shown, but the precise angle is conjectural. The volume of masonry amounts to about 250 m³.

BUILDING PLATFORM

Surviving details in the E, S, and N facades show a three-part format that misleadingly implies presence of three rooms in the building (Fig. 35–38). An upper rear element 0.60 m high appears to sustain the rear part of the building. It is merely a surface articulation of the wall, entirely above the room floor level. The same applies to the middle level in the side insets. These may perhaps be regarded as fake elements. They project an exterior image originally associated with three-room buildings. Perhaps the iconography of the three-part building platform was deemed appropriate for the purpose served by the set of seven structures.

The lower portion has two levels, a frontal body extending laterally about 0.30 m beyond the rear part in S and N facades. Apron moldings with subapron and basal elements elaborate these faces. The apron outset is set almost at mid-height (ratio apron:subapron plus basal molding is 1:0.98). The subapron is 0.33 m high, exactly one quarter of the terrace height. The basal molding, with a height of 0.30 m, represents only slightly less, 23% of terrace height. Batter is 0.15 m in 1.31 m of height; that is, the angle is 7°. The above measurements, taken from the E and S facades, are assumed to apply to the others.

Between these two, within the side inset, is a molding that misleadingly implies existence of a middle room.

BUILDING WALLS

Walls stand full height at the rear and through the side insets. If any frontal wall masonry remains in place it is under debris. The rear wall is exactly 2 m thick, excluding the rear axial outset with a thickness of 0.21 m; the height is 2.2 m. The ratio of thickness to height is 1:1.1, thus, the wall is very nearly as wide as it is high. The two side walls, at the side insets, vary in thickness, from 2 m at the N to 1.64 m at the S. Front walls are assumed thinner, around 1.3 m.

Exterior wall-facing masonry is of veneer type, consistently coursed, and specialized as headers and stretchers. The wall surface has been dressed to a smooth plane following installation of masonry units. Some bits of plaster survive under the medial molding, but there are no traces of paint (Table 4.1).

A standard deviation value of 7.04 indicates a moderate level of standardization in face length of stretchers. Heights are much more controlled to maintain course levels.

The rear facade presents a very clear pattern of scaffolding holes (Fig. 37) in vertically aligned pairs. For construction of the roofcomb, a full scaffolding system would have been necessary.

From evidence at the top of the interior rear wall, it appears the wall-top surface is only a mortar layer, little more than a bed joint in masonry. Some interior plaster survives above debris and no paint is visible.

The single room defined by building walls is set well toward the front. Its width is uncertain; the length is 4.27 m. A single front doorway opening is assumed, although debris profiles give no hint of it.

Volume of masonry in walls totals 75 m³.

Vaulting

Only two courses of vault-soffit facing stones remain in place. They are specialized units, rectangular at the face, shaped to a narrow butt, tapered in section, and well dressed to a smooth face surface after installation (Table 4.2).

Low values of standard deviation indicate a higher level of dimensional control than appears evident for wall-facing masonry.

TABLE 4.1
Structure 5D-93: Exterior Wall Stretcher Dimensions

Dimension	n	Mean (m)	Standard Deviation	Range (m)
Length	78	0.58	7.04	0.31–0.70
Height	78	0.30	1.26	0.27–0.33

TABLE 4.2
Structure 5D-93: Vault-Soffit Header Dimensions

Dimension	n	Mean (m)	Standard Deviation	Range (m)
Face Length	24	0.28	2.17	0.24–0.32
Face Height	24	0.30	3.10	0.25–0.35

Roof and Upper Zones

Upper-zone profiles in the rear part of the building are nearly vertical (Fig. 36–38). At the rear axial outset, the upper-zone surface recedes 0.04 m in a height of 1.61 m. This corresponds to an angle of 1° 30'. The ratio of upper-zone height to wall height is 1:1.37 (73%).

Frontal upper zones are all fallen, and profiles similar to those at the rear are assumed. The three-level arrangement (Fig. 38) reflects building platform data.

The presence of a vault-back surface remains indeterminate. For this reason, upper zone and vault masonry are combined in a volume estimate of 65 m³.

Roofcomb

A stretch of masonry across the rear survives as testimony to the presence of a roofcomb (Fig. 36–38). Extant masonry rises 2.7 m above the upper-zone level, likely about half the original height.

The profile, displaced outward (Fig. 36:1), probably originally rose vertically with a batter of zero degrees.

Masonry volume in the roofcomb is estimated at 80 m³, allowing 10% for a possible chamber, which was not seen in the architectural survey, but noted earlier (Tozzer 1911:142).

Architecture

Three features establish the broad structure type represented by 5D-93 and the other six structures of the Plaza of the Seven Temples. These are the roofcomb, rear axial outset, and side inset. Subcategories may be established on the basis of relatively small size, the presence of a single room, and a single front doorway.

Attributes that can be considered as "late" at Tikal include veneer wall facing, the building platform apron molding, near-vertical upper-zone profile, and (conjectural) fully outset stair. Relatively low upper zones in relation to wall height may emerge as an "early" attribute (Table 4.3).

TABLE 4.3
Structure 5D-93: Time Spans

Time Span	Comment
1	Period of abandonment and collapse.
2	Period of occupancy as originally built.
3	Period of construction, approximately 470 m³ of masonry.

V

Structure 5D-94

Second from S in the row of Seven Temples, Str. 5D-94 faces toward the W onto the Plaza (Fig. 1). Rear elements of building platform, building, and roofcomb stand above collapse debris. Upper parts of the roofcomb and frontal elements have fallen. Nagy in 1964 and 1965 and Orrego in 1968 did the recording under the architectural survey program, which was focused on recording data available with minimal clearing and excavation.

Previous studies do not mention this structure. The Tozzer/Merwin map (Tozzer 1911) shows it as number 57, apparently on a separate platform together with their number 56 (our 5D-93). These two structures are freestanding, although the five others abut terracing associated with the South Acropolis.

Based on rear wall lines, cardinal orientation is 9°, 10' W of magnetic N (for 1964). The mean declination presented in TR. 11 for 1960 puts this at 2°, 25' E of true N (2°, 25' N of W).

Construction Stages

There are no formal pause-lines marked by plaster surfaces installed on completion of a stage prior to commencement of the next stage. Apparently, workers assembled the structure in one continuous operation. Despite this, exterior architectural forms are designed to project an appearance of distinct stages. These are discussed below as substages.

Lower Substructure Platform, Building Platform, and Building Walls

LOWER SUBSTRUCTURE PLATFORM

Judging from the plan of the building platform, it seems likely that the lower substructure platform is in two parts of equal height (Fig. 40–44). The frontal part is shown as wider than the rear. This is conjectural and the amount of projection is utter guesswork.

A surface accessed by excavation is assumed to be the rear axial outset apron. Apron moldings are assumed on other parts of the platform. Stair width is estimated from debris contours, but the number of risers is unknown.

A modest excavation (Op. 116) established the lower substructure platform height as 3.7 m. This amounts to 26% of the total (reconstructed) height. Estimated masonry is 300 m³. Terrace-facing masonry at this location appears very similar to wall-facing masonry.

BUILDING PLATFORM

Although the building has side insets, the building platform lacks this feature. Its top steps up from front to rear in three levels. The upper level looks like a separate platform standing on the lower level and sustaining the rear part of the building. But, since the room floor is at the level of the top of the lower part of the building platform, this upper part is merely a molding applied to the wall face. The middle level appears in the side inset of the building and it, too, is a mere molding, not the face of a body of core material.

Frontal elements of the lower part of the building platform extend laterally beyond rear elements with no step-up. A three-part apron molding runs around the lower part except at the rear axial outset, where there is only a two-part molding with no basal element. Elsewhere, the molding employs apron, subapron, and basal elements.

The apron represents 58% of the height of the lower part of the building platform. The subapron accounts for 25%, and the basal molding, 17%. Batter, as measured at the rear axial outset, is 8°.

A mini-stair of four risers is assumed at the front, but not indicated by debris contours.

Masonry volume is approximately 50 m³.

BUILDING WALLS

At the rear, the apparent wall height measures 2.2 m. But since the basal molding is really part of the wall and stands above floor level in the room (Fig. 41), the true wall height is 2.85 m. Thickness, excluding the rear axial outset, is 1.83 m, and this results in a thickness-to-height ratio of 1:1.56. The thinner front wall measures 1.33 m in thickness for a height of 2.35 m (ratio value is 1:1.77).

At the rear axial outset the exterior wall face has a batter of 3°. Similar batter occurs at the N outset return face. Other accessible wall faces have zero batter. Wall planes are smooth, and dressed to a true surface after installation of masonry. Facings are rectangular veneer units that are well shaped, specialized as headers and stretchers, and consistently

coursed (Table 5.1).

Scaffolding holes appear in rear and N facades and several of these are sealed with primary plaster. The wall top is not plastered, however. Traces of exterior plaster survive in the medial outset and interior surfaces are plaster covered; no traces of paint remain.

Walls enclose a single room whose length is 3.1 times its width. Room area is 16% of gross building area.

Walls encompass a masonry volume of approximately 75 m³.

Vaulting

Only a small portion of the room vault remains in place (Fig. 41). Soffit stones here are rectangular with the greater dimension in the vertical and coursing appears continuous. The soffit face has been dressed to a smooth, regular plane following masonry installation. Capstones are preplastered (Table 5.2).

A vault-back surface may exist, concealed by debris. Because of this problem, the volume of masonry employed in vaulting is indeterminate and lumped together (below) with upper zones and roof volume.

Upper Zones and Roof

The only surviving upper-zone surface is at the rear and here there are no medial or superior moldings (Fig. 40–44). Frontal upper zones have been similarly reconstructed, merely through lack of evidence. In many cases at Tikal rear upper zones lack moldings while frontal elements have them. Rear

TABLE 5.1
Structure 5D-94: Wall-Facing Stretcher Dimensions

Dimension	n	Mean (m)	Standard Deviation	Range (m)
Ext. Face Length	100	0.59	9.04	0.30–0.72
Ext. Face Height	100	0.30	3.19	0.27–0.41
Int. Face Length	4	0.53	8.35	0.40–0.63
Int. Face Height	4	0.29	2.49	0.25–0.32

TABLE 5.2
Structure 5D-94: Vault-Soffit Facing Dimensions

Dimension	n	Mean (m)	Standard Deviation	Range (m)
Face Length	7	0.23	2.47	0.19–0.26
Face Height	7	0.25	1.91	0.22–0.27

upper-zone height is 63% of wall height. This may emerge as anachronistically "early."

Masonry volume in upper zones and vaults amounts to approximately 65 m³.

Roofcomb

Enough material remains in place at the rear to establish existence of a roofcomb. Original height is problematic and is perhaps twice the surviving height, or about 4 m. The presence of a chamber cannot be determined without excavation. As a rough estimate, masonry volume might total about 65 m³.

Relationship to Adjacent Stratigraphy

The lower substructure platform rests on a hard-surfaced, well-made floor. At the rear, a second floor abuts the subapron, but its status as primary or secondary is unclear.

Architecture

Large families of structures at Tikal present a particular suite of features: roofcomb, rear axial outset, and side inset (Fig. 45a,b). Structure 5D-94 clearly falls into this category, in a subclass of examples with single front doorway and single room.

Properties that appear "late" in the history of building at Tikal include veneer facings, wall-top plaster, post-dressing, three-part apron moldings, relatively thick walls, room area small in relation to gross building area, and fully outset stair. One possible "early" feature is the somewhat low upper-zone height in relation to wall height (Table 5.3).

TABLE 5.3
Structure 5D-94: Time Spans

Time Span	Operation	Comment
1		Period of abandonment and collapse.
2	116	Period of occupancy as originally built.
3		Period of construction, approximately 550 m³ of masonry.

VI

Structure 5D-95

When Tikal authorities commissioned the Seven Temples, there must have been a pressing need for space in the Plaza; five of the structures crowd back onto a terrace of the South Acropolis so that some of their lower parts either abut its face or have been partially obscured by it. The situation is particularly awkward for 5D-95 because it partially abuts the terrace and partially extends beyond it. South, E, and N facades all impinge upon it.

The stratigraphic relationship remains unclear because collapse debris obscures all junctures (Fig. 51). Reconstructions illustrated in Fig. 46–50 assume prior existence of the South Acropolis terrace, but this relationship is still to be established. In any case, intersections between 5D-95 and the South Acropolis terrace must be approximately as shown regardless of sequence.

The recording done by Nagy and Orrego for the Tikal Standing Architectural Survey was done in 1964, 1965, and 1968. Previous studies discuss the Seven Temples Group but do not specifically mention 5D-95. As with the other six, frontal parts have fallen to below the debris surface. Rear parts are free-standing, partially intact, with upper portions fallen. Frontal orientation is to the W. Cardinal orientation, based on rear wall lines, bears 7° W of magnetic N. That is less than 1° W of true N as established for the Tikal Project base maps (TR. 11).

Construction Stages

The survey failed to detect any formalized pause-lines. There appear to be no plastered top surfaces intervening between components such as building platform and walls, or walls and vaults. Therefore, the elements of exterior architectural form that normally equate to construction stages at Tikal do not do so here. Some parts may have been under construction while others, apparently sustaining them, had not been entirely completed. The standard set of architectural "parts" follows, but they must be considered here as mere substages.

Lower Substructure Platform, Building Platform, and Building Walls

LOWER SUBSTRUCTURE PLATFORM

Debris entirely conceals the (assumed) lower substructure platform (Fig. 46–50). Estimated height is approximately 3.5 m. On the basis of the building platform layout, the lower component is depicted in two parts, the front part wider than the rear. Debris profiles suggest the presence of an outset stair. All details illustrated in the figures are predictions, and estimated volume of masonry is 330 m³.

BUILDING PLATFORM

Three members of the building platform are present (Fig. 46–50). The lower is a platform 1.2 m high. It extends from front to rear at one level, the front part wider than the rear. Sides, front, and lateral elements of the rear facade present three-part apron profiles. Both 5D-93 and 94 have a two-part apron at the rear axial outset. The same arrangement is predicted here. Apron batter, measurable at the SW corner, is 5°. Apron height is 58% and subapron height is 25% of terrace height; the basal molding is 8% of terrace height.

The middle level, within the side insets, is merely a molding, not related to any room floor level or any body of core material other than the wall core. Its height is 0.30 m.

The upper level, presenting itself as the support for the rear part of the building, is 0.60 m high with nearly zero batter. Because the building has two rooms, the rear room floor is assumed to coincide with the top of this subcomponent. Whether this is true will emerge when the rooms are eventually cleared of collapse debris.

Volume of masonry contained in building platform components totals approximately 100 m³.

BUILDING WALLS

On the assumption that the upper subcomponent of the building platform coincides with the rear room floor level, the wall stands 2.4 m high (Fig. 46–50). Thickness, exclusive of the rear axial outset, is 2.3 m, that is, the wall section is very nearly square. Elsewhere around the building wall thickness varies.

Both interior and exterior facings employ thin rectangular veneer stones specialized as headers and stretchers in regular courses. Wall planes have been dressed to a smooth surface after installation of facing masonry. No plaster survives except on interior surfaces (Table 6.1).

Walls enclose two rooms, the front room not directly measurable, but evidently larger than the inner room. Total room area amounts to 23% of gross area. Rear-room proportion is 1:3.6.

Level changes in the top surface of building platform subcomponents imply a step-up from the front room to the rear room. This is another feature to be verified by excavation.

Wall construction represents 130 m³ of masonry.

Vaults and Upper Zones

A lintel bed is visible at the N jamb of the doorway to the inner room; lintel installation would initiate vault construction. No lintel details survive. Vault soffits have straight-line profiles, which are rather irregular, and soffit pitch is 19°. Capstones are preplastered. The vault-back surface is not visible and its existence is not established (Table 6.2).

The upper zone at the rear axial outset has no medial molding. The pitch is 4.5° and the upper height at this location is 71% of wall height.

A medial molding is visible at the S side inset. This might mean that frontal upper zones have medial moldings, but no evidence survives. No roof surface is evident.

Vaults and upper zones represent approximately 100 m³ of masonry.

Roofcomb

Masonry of the roofcomb survives almost 3 m above the upper-zone level at the rear axial outset. Full height is assumed to be similar to that of other structures in the group. This yields a masonry volume of approximately 120 m³, assuming absence of a chamber.

TABLE 6.1
Structure 5D-95: Stretcher Dimensions, Walls

Dimension	n	Mean (m)	Standard Deviation	Range (m)
Ext. Length	77	0.58	6.86	0.30–0.68
Ext. Height	77	0.31	1.39	0.27–0.34
Int. Length	7	0.53	7.26	0.40–0.60
Int. Height	7	0.29	1.76	0.26–0.31

Relationship to Adjacent Stratigraphy

Rear elements of 5D-95 engage with the W face of a terrace connected with the South Acropolis. Whether the terrace precedes or follows the structure remains unresolved.

Architecture

Structures possessing three features—rear axial outset, side inset, and roofcomb—form a distinct morphological category at Tikal. Structure 5D-95 represents a subcategory within this class defined by two rooms arranged in tandem, and perhaps, by its modest size.

Visible aspects of architectural form and masonry attributes, specifically ashlar exterior wall facings, indicate a "late" date in the history of masonry construction at Tikal. By contrast, erecting the whole building component in one continuous operation is more typical of "early" work. An unusual feature visible in the inner room is the unequal height of vault springs. Only a few other structures at Tikal present this condition (Table 6.3).

TABLE 6.2
Structure 5D-95: Vault-Soffit Facing Dimensions

Dimension	n	Mean (m)	Standard Deviation	Range (m)
Face Length*	22	0.25	2.77	0.20–0.29
Face Height*	22	0.31	2.56	0.26–0.36
Face Length**	7	0.25	1.69	0.23–0.28
Face Height**	7	0.28	1.83	0.25–0.30

*in half-vault units
**in end-vault units

TABLE 6.3
Structure 5D-95: Time Spans

Time Span	Comment
1	Period of abandonment and collapse.
2	Period of occupancy as originally built.
3	Period of construction, approximately 800 m³ of masonry.

VII

Structure 5D-96

This is the central of seven structures on the E edge of the Plaza of the Seven Temples. It is higher than the other six and the only one adorned with sculptural panels. Like the others, its frontal (W) parts have fallen and everything below building level lies buried under collapse debris. On axis in front, St. P37 and Alt. P31 poke through the forest litter. These features, in particular, emphasize the dominant central status of 5D-96.

Rear exterior wall lines, the only features accessible for this purpose, determine cardinal orientation as 3.5° W of magnetic N; that is, 3°, 15' E of true N as established for the Tikal Project base maps (TR. 11).

Maler photographed the rear facade (1911:fig. 2, pl. 8) and described it in detail. His photograph shows something that may be a sculptural panel at roofcomb level in the rear axial outset. This surface has degraded since his time and no panel is now visible. Tozzer prepared a plan (1911:fig. 37) that agrees with our plan (Fig. 52), except that we show the single room as a little wider. In both cases, room width is largely guesswork.

In the Tikal Standing Architectural Survey by Nagy (1965 season) and Orrego (1968 season), nearly all observations are of features standing above debris. Two small trenches at the rear of the building provide data not visible on the surface.

Construction Stages

Surfaces indicative of pauses in the process of construction are not visible. Therefore, only one construction stage can be defined. This must include all morphological components from lower basal platform to roofcomb. As a result, the various "parts" discussed below are all substages.

Lower Substructure Platform, Building Platform, and Building Walls

LOWER SUBSTRUCTURE PLATFORM

On the basis of (estimated) building platform height (frontal part assumed), the lower substructure platform is roughly 5 m high (Fig. 52–54). Presumably, it abuts the W face of a terrace associated with the South Acropolis. Figures 52, 53, and 54 illustrate a line of abutment by rough extrapolation from debris contours. From these assumptions the masonry volume, including the stair presumed from the debris profile, is calculated to be 450 m³.

BUILDING PLATFORM

A feature presenting the appearance of a building platform was exposed in two small excavations at the rear (Fig. 52–55). Probably it is no more than a basal molding applied to the rear wall face. That is, its top level is probably well above the room floor level (Fig. 53). It projects the appearance of a building platform, but corresponds to no body of core material except for wall core. Therefore, it is referred to here as a fake building platform. Its height is almost exactly 1 m and its batter is very slight, 3°.

A genuine building platform probably exists at a lower level (Fig. 54). Figure 54 shows a conjectural apron profile and frontal stair. Assumed height is 1.5 m. Masonry volume totals (very roughly) 100 m³.

Building Walls

Rear axial outset and side insets are known from rearward parts that rise above debris (Fig. 52). Frontal parts are estimated. Gross area is 101 m². Room area is estimated as 14 m², or 14% of gross area. Rear wall thickness is assumed to equate with the position of the rear return wall facet at the side inset. This yields a thickness of 3.6 m.

Rear wall height is problematic. Apparent wall height, seen on the exterior from the top of the fake building platform to the medial molding, is 2.6 m. But if the fake building platform is regarded as merely a basal molding on the wall face, then wall height is 3.6 m. Batter is zero or slightly negative, although this might be an effect of slumping.

Exterior wall-facing masonry consists of rectangular, veneer-type stones consistently coursed and specialized as headers and stretchers. The latter predominate in frequency. Face dimensions are relatively highly standardized and face surfaces have been planed to a smooth finish following masonry installation. Principal rear corners are rounded to a radius of ca. 0.15 m. Other corners are more sharply cut (Table 7.1).

The low value of standard deviation for face height expresses regularity of coursing. Inset panels are visible on three wall faces at the rear of the building (Fig. 52–55). Side channels are ca. 0.15 m deep. Figure 54 presents an inset panel on a frontal wall facet, but this is entirely conjectural.

Scaffolding holes are visible across the rear facade and in the rear portions of N and S facades. These probably are upper members of vertically aligned pairs, the lower members concealed by debris.

Exterior wall plaster survives under the medial molding at the rear. No paint is evident. The condition of the wall top, whether plastered or not plastered, was not noted. Volume of masonry in walls is approximately 310 m³.

Vaulting

The single room vault has completely fallen. A rough estimate of masonry volume amounts to 300 m³.

Upper Zones

Only the rear upper zones survive. In the N and S facades, only rearward portions remain. These elements all contain sculptural features (Fig. 54–61). In the rear facade, most of the central sculptural element has been lost.

The two side panels (N and S facades) present similar motifs with minor but probably significant differences. Central elements of each are frontal skull images. The S skull is curiously split. Perhaps it can be read as two profile views making a frontal image. At the N, the skull image is clearly frontal, but the middle part has fallen. From the arrangement of surviving teeth there does not appear to be room for a split image similar to that on the S. Eye images occupy corner and center positions in both panels. On the S, all the eyes look upwards and downwards. On the N, they look E and W except for the vertically oriented central pair. Between the eye images are crossed bones essentially similar in both panels.

The rear facade sculpture involves three panels, a central one on the rear axial outset and two flanking panels (Fig. 58–61). The flanking panels are crossed bones, identical at first glance but subtly different on closer inspection. The crossed bone images are actually mesh units, a device very widespread in Meso-

TABLE 7.1
Structure 5D-96: Exterior Wall Masonry, Face Dimensions

Dimension	n	Mean (m)	Standard Deviation	Range (m)
Face Length	100	0.57	6.03	0.32–0.70
Face Height	100	0.30	1.28	0.26–0.33

american iconography. On the S panel, the upright "vee" of the mesh moves from behind to in front of the inverted vee (scanning left to right). This is reversed in the N panel.

The central panel has a badly preserved middle motif flanked by two large squarish "eye" images with hooked irises. Surrounding them are other "eye" images in corner positions with motifs that slightly resemble Venus glyphs between them. The overall form is most typical of shields in Maya art.

Figures 54–57a, 58, and 59a illustrating sculptural features are rendered in single-line technique that somewhat misrepresents the lapidary treatment. As Fig. 57b, 59b, and 61 show, they are carved as rounded forms not quite so sharp edged. Erosion and weathering have further blurred the detail. No doubt they were originally painted, but no trace of either paint or plaster remains.

Upper-zone height at the rear is almost exactly 2 m and essentially vertical across the rear facade, but with moderate batter on the sides. Ratio of wall height (including the fake building platform) to upper-zone height is 1:0.77.

Because of the distance between interior and exterior wall surfaces, upper-zone masonry occupies a relatively large volume. This is estimated as approximately 100 m³.

Roofcomb

Although it is partially standing at the rear, all the front part of the roofcomb has fallen away (Fig. 53–55, 61). Estimated height above upper-zone level is 6 m. Rear facings have slumped outward. The reconstructed rear profile has moderate batter. A panel of some sort may have been present at about the mid-height center of the rear axial outset (Tozzer 1911:pl. 8). The volume of masonry is estimated at 220 m³, assuming absence of a chamber.

Architecture

Diagnostic morphological features include rear axial outset, side insets, relatively modest size, single room, and fake building platform. Attributes suggestive of a "late" date of construction include veneer masonry, relatively thick building walls, and a relatively shallow projection of outsets. Potentially "early" attributes include the ratio of upper-zones height to wall height, and presence of inset panels in the building walls.

Relationship to Adjacent Stratigraphy

Limited excavations at the rear of the building revealed a floor running under the fake building platform. A thin skim coat overlies this floor, which is primary to 5D-96, and there are two other surfaces: a 0.10 m thick floor overlies this skim coat and abuts the fake building platform, and a 3 cm floor overlies it and also abuts the fake building platform. All but the primary floor appear associated with the South Acropolis (Table 7.2).

TABLE 7.2
Structure 5D-96: Time Spans

Time Span	Comment
1	Period of abandonment and collapse.
2	Period of use as initially built. During this period, two floors associated with the South Acropolis were laid against the rear facade.
3	Period of initial construction, approximately 1,400 m³ of masonry.

VIII

Structure 5D-97

Were it not one of the Seven Temples, the architectural survey would have bypassed this structure, immediately N of center in the group of seven (Fig. 1). It is little more than a mound of collapse debris. Only a small portion of the N side inset and the rear wall facet on the N side remain unencumbered. A small exposure of vaulting, slightly amplified by modest excavation, provides the only other detail accessible without excavation. Nevertheless, with modest conjecture, the main lines of the structure can be extrapolated from these few visible features. The structure faces W with cardinal orientation, implied by the limited accessible features, 3.6° W of magnetic N.

Nagy (1965 season) and Orrego (1968 season) recorded the architectural information (Tikal Standing Architecture Survey). Figures 62, 63, and 64 illustrate the structure most likely to emerge on removal of collapse debris.

Construction Stages

Broken-line extensions of extant features are based on the other structures of the group. They assume the presence of a lower substructure platform, a building platform, a building, and a roofcomb. Since no details of these components are specific to 5D-97, they are not discussed below. Plastered pause-lines are not evident. The parts that normally correspond to construction stages in "late" work here are classified as substages.

Building

BUILDING WALLS

Exterior wall configuration includes a side inset partially visible on the N facade (Fig. 62–64). This detail determines a two-part exterior format, the front part wider than the rear part. Wall-facing masonry is of veneer type, but not enough units for statistical sampling are available. There is a vaulted room and from the half-vault dimensions its width must be approximately 1.3 m. Some interior plaster remains under the vault spring. There is no evidence of paint and the wall top is not plastered.

Vaulting

The one surviving half-vault (Fig. 63) is four courses high. The uppermost course is much lower than the others, probably a leveling course. The soffit angle is 27.5°. The face of the soffit has been dressed to a smooth, regular plane following masonry installation. Capstones are preplastered. The small surface exposed does not include any vault-beam sockets.

Roofcomb

Material above capstone level, though concealed beneath collapse debris, is sufficient to indicate the presence of a roofcomb.

Architecture

It is assumed that 5D-97 is similar to the other members of the Seven Temples. No visible feature contradicts this. Veneer-type exterior wall-facing masonry and vault masonry indicate a relatively late date of construction.

Relationship to Adjacent Stratigraphy

Presumably 5D-97 abuts a preexisting terrace associated with the South Acropolis. Figures 62–64 present an assumed line of abutment (Table 8.1).

TABLE 8.1
Structure 5D-97: Time Spans

Time Span	Comment
1	Period of abandonment and collapse.
2	Period of occupancy.
3	Period of construction, approximately 500 m³ of masonry.

Structure 5D-98

Second from the N end of the line of Seven Temples (Fig. 1), collapse debris conceals most extant features of Str. 5D-98 and many parts appear to have fallen completely. Rear side-wall facets, side insets, the N facet of the rear wall, some interior walls, and some vault surfaces are partially accessible. Although a roofcomb is assumed comparable to other members of the group, the volume of debris seems inadequate (Fig. 65). Nagy did the Tikal Standing Architectural Survey in 1964 and 1965.

The structure faces toward the W. Cardinal orientation, based on rear wall lines, bears 1°, 10' W of magnetic N (5°, 35' E of true N), as established for the Tikal base maps (TR. 11).

Construction Stages

Since the only visible features are wall and vault elements, they are the only ones discussed. Presumably the structure includes a lower substructure platform, a building platform, upper zones, and a roofcomb. Pause-lines marked by plaster levels appear absent. Therefore, the various components are classified as substages. Calculations of masonry volume are based on estimated dimensions.

Building

BUILDING WALLS

The walls enclose a single room of known length, but uncertain width, although the half-vault provides a good estimate (Fig. 65, 66). Rear wall thickness is 2.75 m, exclusive of the (assumed) rear axial outset. Wall heights are estimated and the wall top, at the one accessible location, lacks plaster.

Veneer-type stones face interior and exterior wall surfaces. They are consistently coursed and specialized as headers and stretchers. Wall facets have been dressed to smooth, regular surfaces following masonry setting. No plaster remains (Table 9.1).

The high value for interior face length is mainly due to the small sample size.

TABLE 9.1
Structure 5D-98: Face Dimensions of Wall-Facing Stones

Dimension	n	Mean (m)	Standard Deviation	Range (m)
Ext. Length	34	0.54	8.12	0.29–0.65
Ext. Height	34	0.30	4.24	0.18–0.42

Vaulting

The surviving half-vault (Fig. 65) presents a straight-line profile four courses high and smoothly dressed, following installation of masonry. The soffit angle is 28°. The top course, lower than the others, probably served to level the capstones and, therefore, has not been included in the sample of dimensions. No surviving plaster is visible (Table 9.2).

Roofcomb

Material above capstone level seems more than accountable for upper-zone masonry and, therefore, probably signifies existence of a roofcomb that has fallen almost completely (Fig. 65). Any surface details that may remain are obscured by debris.

Architecture

Presence of side insets places 5D-98 in a category defined by structures with this feature. Rear axial outsets normally accompany side insets, but in this case debris obscures this feature. Veneer-type facing stones imply a relatively "late" date of construction.

Relationship to Adjacent Stratigraphy

Construction workers probably built 5D-98 up against a preexisting terrace associated with the South Acropolis. This condition is established for 5D-96 and assumed valid here. Only about 0.60 m of the rear wall stands above this terrace. The diagonal line of abutment (Fig. 65, 67) is an estimated datum (Table 9.3).

TABLE 9.2
Structure 5D-98: Vault-Soffit Header Dimensions

Dimension	n	Mean (m)	Standard Deviation	Range (m)
Length*	12	0.27	1.6	0.24–0.31
Height*	12	0.27	2.85	0.22–0.33
Length**	6	0.27	1.37	0.25–0.29
Height**	6	0.27	1.89	0.24–0.29

*Half-Vault
**End-Vault

TABLE 9.3
Structure 5D-98: Time Spans

Time Span	Comment
1	Period of abandonment and collapse.
2	Period of occupancy.
3	Period of construction, approximately 450 m³ of masonry.

X

Structure 5D-99

In the SW quadrant of the site center, the E side of the eponymously named Plaza of the Seven Temples is defined by a row of seven structures. From their similarity and arrangement, the seven appear to represent a single architectural project. Structure 5D-99 stands at the N end of the row (Fig. 1).

Nagy recorded architectural data in 1964 and 1965 under the Tikal Standing Architectural Survey terms of reference. The intent of this program was to obtain data available on the surface. For this purpose, some underbrush was cleared away, but no excavation disturbed the debris surface covering large parts of the structure.

Frontal orientation of the structure is toward the W. Cardinal orientation, based on rear wall lines, bears 4° W of magnetic N (2°, 45' W of true N) as determined for the Tikal Project base maps (TR. 11).

Construction Stages

In effect, there is only one construction stage. That is, the structure appears to have been built in a single operation uninterrupted by significant pauses. Although only some facets of wall and vault masonry are visible above debris, the structure most likely includes a lower substructure platform, upper zones, and a roofcomb. These components, either fallen or covered with debris, are illustrated speculatively (Fig. 68, 69). They appear to represent construction stages, but are classified as substages because evidence for completion of each prior to commencement of the next appears lacking.

Lower Substructure Platform, Building Platform, and Building Walls

LOWER SUBSTRUCTURE PLATFORM

The only firm datum for the lower substructure platform is height, approximately 4 m based on the estimated level of the Plaza floor. A front stair is implied by debris contours. Stair details illustrated are conjectural.

BUILDING PLATFORM

Exterior features visible at the sides of the structure present the image of a three-element building platform. Two of these "parts" are merely articulations of wall surface; they do not correspond to a body of material sustaining walls. Since this is precisely the impression they convey, they may be considered as fake building platform elements.

The lower, frontal part is a genuine building platform in that it actually does sustain the walls. An apron molding with subapron and basal elements articulates the surface. The height, 1.40 m, implies presence of a stair. The stair illustrated is merely hypothetical.

BUILDING WALLS

Exterior wall facets include side insets and turnouts for an eroded rear axial outset (Fig. 68). Thickness of the rear wall, excluding the rear axial outset, is 2.2 m. Thickness-to-height ratio is 1:1.14. Lateral walls in the frontal part of the building are 2.60 m thick. Thickness here actually exceeds height (2.50 m). Front wall thickness is estimated.

Veneer-type stones specialized as headers and stretchers, consistently coursed, form both exterior and interior facings. Mortar joints are thin and spalls absent. Wall facets have been dressed to a regular surface following masonry installation and corners are distinctly rounded (Table 10.1).

The surface running under the walls is not plastered. The wall top, similarly, lacks a plaster finish.

Vaulting

Visible vault elements have outset springs. Soffit profiles are straight-line, and four courses high. The top course is a leveling course of reduced height. The half-vault soffit angle is 28.5°. Face surfaces have been smoothed to a regular profile and the dressing for this followed masonry installation. The capstones are preplastered.

Upper Zones

On the two side facades, medial molding outsets are visible but no upper-zone details survive. Height, profile, and surface treatment are all speculative. No moldings are shown, but this does not mean absence of moldings.

Roofcomb

Material above vault-cap level indicates the presence of a roofcomb, but no details are available and most of it has fallen.

Architecture

The architectural category that includes 5D-99 is defined by the presence of side insets and the almost certain presence of a rear axial outset. Tikal Report 34A presents the full membership and range of attribute variation for this class. Veneer-type facing stones imply a relatively late date of construction. Absence of plaster surfaces between construction stages is an attribute of early construction and, in this case, it may be an intentional archaism. The function served by these seven structures may have had unusually strong associations with older traditions.

Relationship to Adjacent Stratigraphy

By inference from the other members of the Seven Temples, 5D-99 probably was built up against a preexisting terrace associated with the South Acropolis. This relationship is demonstrable for 5D-96 only. In all cases the precise line of abutment is estimated (Table 10.2).

TABLE 10.1
Structure 5D-99: Face Dimensions of Wall Facing Stretchers

Dimension	n	Mean (m)	Standard Deviation	Range (m)
Ext. Length	39	0.59	7.59	0.31–0.71
Ext. Height	39	0.29	2.70	0.21–0.34
Int. Length	4	0.56	11.54	0.36–0.66
Int. Height	5	0.28	1.72	0.25–0.30

TABLE 10.2
Structure 5D-99: Time Spans

Time Span	Comment
1	Period of abandonment and collapse.
2	Period of occupancy.
3	Period of construction, approximately 540 m^3 of masonry.

Conclusions

Based on masonry characteristics such as veneer facings, the nine structures comprising 5D-91 through 99 all appear to be Late Classic works, possibly representing only two episodes of construction. On the S side of the Plaza of the Seven Temples, three structures, 5D-90 through 92, may have been designed and built as one development. Similarly, seven structures on the E side, 5D-93 through 99, look like one architectural composition. In both cases, this assessment reflects symmetry of arrangement. In each series (three structures in the one case and seven in the other), a larger work stands at the center so that each has a distinctly unified appearance.

With the limited information provided by surface survey, no sequence is evident between these two sets of structures, and whether they represent early or late developments within the Late Classic period is not known.

Structure 5D-91 occupies part of the SW edge of the epicenter of Tikal and has large impressive stairs on both sides. It provides for formal passage from a zone where people walk on mere dirt to one where they stand on plaster paving. At the E end of the epicenter, where the East Plaza and with it a great market is based, it seems likely that ordinary people could come and go. Those entering through 5D-91 had to climb up a high stair, pass through a vaulted building, and then descend the same vertical distance; these may not have been ordinary people. The formality of this entry implies something of an official nature, not merely using facilities of the epicenter, but joining with the elite caste who may have lived there full time, claiming a connection with deceased ancestors and natural forces.

If this speculative assessment is at all accurate, the nature of the sculptural imagery on the building may come into focus. Although badly decayed, the high-relief figures at the four corners of the upper zone show realistic human features, delicately modeled, and surrounded by status symbols. The larger masks centered on both sides of the roof structure also look human, though only the lower features (mouth and chin) remain in place.

These figures may have concisely identified those inhabitants of the epicenter who knew the iconography, as well as those entering by this formal portal. The cumbersome devices allowing the doorways on both sides to be closed suggest that the building was indeed closed for extended periods. It may have been personages rather than mere people who entered this way, and only occasionally at that. Magnitude, magnificence, and brilliant display provide clues across the centuries that inhabitation of the epicenter carried great meaning and value for the life of the city as a whole. Tikal might have been occupied by two very distinct classes—those residing within the epicenter and those in the rest of the city.

Structures 5D-90, 91, and 92 may have been designed and built as a single complex—the symmetry of the three structures suggests this. If so, then 90 and 92 might have served as support facilities for the central, more monumental structure (5D-91). There could have been a sizeable establishment dedicated to managing the sort of formal entry that the complex served.

Structures 5D-90 and 5D-91 may have been identical in format. Structure 5D-90 has collapsed too completely for this to be certain, but the debris mound is consistent with it. Compositions of this kind are rare at Tikal. Early Classic Str. 5D-23 and 24 on the North Acropolis, Preclassic Sub.1-1st and Sub.9, 5E-34 and 35, and Late Classic 5E-33 and 36 in the East Plaza may have formed identical pairs. These are very different kinds of architecture, indicating that pairing could be done in quite different contexts, though not often and widely spread out in time. Speculatively, paired formats might imply functional unity. This certainly seems likely in the East Plaza cases, and thus possibly extends to the two others as well.

It may be no accident that 5D-91 provides formal entry to the Plaza of the Seven Temples. These seven also seem to have been designed as one complex, lining the E side of the Plaza. Relief sculpture on the central structure of the group, 5D-96, is as different as can be from 5D-91. Here we find no human imagery. The figures are skulls, crossed bones, and grotesque masks–the language of the non-human. The criterion for residence within the epicenter, together with lineage, might have been a claimed connection between human and non-human.

The seven structures 5D-93 through 99 can be classified with reasonable certainty as temples and are nearly identical in form, though there are some surprising differences among them. Their temple diagnostics include essentially vertical format (though not really high), and rear axial outsets. The latter feature is regarded here as the most reliable temple diagnostic at Tikal. All the Great Temples have rear axial outsets, as do all the structures on the North Acropolis. An exception is 5D-66 in the Central Acropolis, which seems temple-like but lacks the rear axial outset.

Surmised is that structures with rear axial outsets were designed as places that could be occupied by non-human entities, forces of nature, and celestial beings. Anyone entering the epicenter formally through 5D-91 would have belonged to the epicenter caste and, therefore, a space dominated by the architecture of the non-human moiety might have been part of the entry ceremony. Members of the epicenter caste who had been out of the area perhaps had to purify themselves again on reentry, and the seven temples could have served this function.

References

Gómez, Oswaldo

2006   El Proyecto Plaza de los Siete Templos de Tikal: Nuevas intervenciones. In *XIX Simposio de Investigaciones Arqueológicas en Guatemala, 2005*, edited by J.P. Laporte, B. Arroyo, and H. Mejía, pp. 768–89. Guatemala City: Museo Nacional de Arqueología y Etnología.

2007   Proyecto Plaza de Los Siete Templos de Tikal: Los Edificios del Sur de la Plaza. In *XX Simposio de Investigaciones Arqueológicas en Guatemala, 2006*, edited by J.P. Laporte, B, Arroyo, and H. Mejía, pp. 492–518. Guatemala City: Museo Nacional de Arqueología y Etnología.

2008   El Proyecto Plaza de los Siete Templos de Tikal: Excavación de los Templos al este de la Plaza. In *XXI Simposio de Investigaciones Arqueológicas en Guatemala, 2007*, edited by J.P. Laporte, B, Arroya, and H. Mejía, pp. 544–55. Guatemala City: Museo Nacional de Arqueología y Etnología.

2013   *Nuevos Datos para la Historia de Tikal*. Serie de Estudios Arqueológicas 8. Guatemala City: Dirección General del Patrimonio Cultural y Natural.

Maler, Teobert

1911   *Explorations in the Department of Peten, Guatemala*. Memoirs of the Peabody Museum of Archaeology and Ethnology vol. 5 no. 1. Cambridge, MA: Peabody Museum of Archaeology and Ethnology, Harvard University.

Thompson, J. Eric S.

1950   *Maya Hieroglyphic Writing: Introduction*. Washington, DC: Carnegie Institute of Washington Publication 589.

Tozzer, Alfred M.

1911   *Preliminary Study of the Ruins of Tikal, Guatemala*. Memoirs of the Peabody Museum of Archaeology and Ethnology vol. 5 no. 2. Cambridge, MA: Peabody Museum of Archaeology and Ethnology, Harvard University.

Tikal Reports (see TR. 12):
TR. 11:
Carr, Robert F., and James E. Hazard

1961   Map of the Ruins of Tikal, El Peten, Guatemala. In *Tikal Reports 1–11*, edited by E.M. Shook, W.R. Coe, V.L. Broman, and L. Satterthwaite, pp. iii-26. Facsimile Reissue of 1986 of Original Reports Published 1958–1961. Philadelphia: The University Museum, University of Pennsylvania.

TR. 31:

Trik, Helen, and Michael E. Kampen

1983   *The Graffiti of Tikal*. Philadelphia: The University Museum, University of Pennsylvania.

TR. 34A:

Loten, H. Stanley

2007   *A Commentary on the Architecture of the North Acropolis, Tikal, Guatemala: Additions and Alterations, Part A*. Philadelphia: University of Pennsylvania Museum of Archaeology and Anthropology.

Illustrations

FIGURE 1

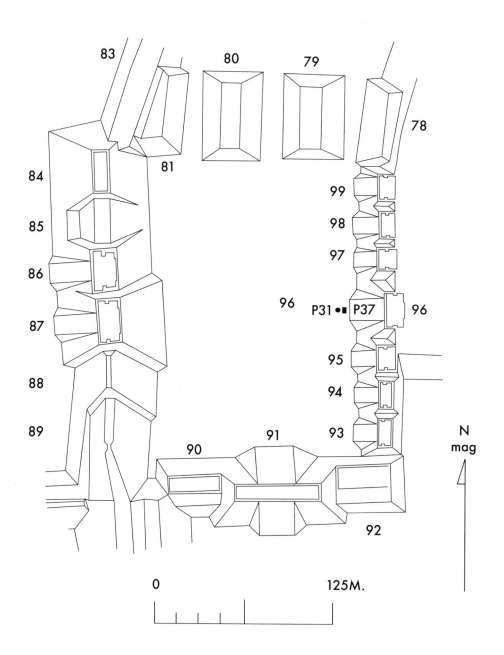

Map of the Plaza of the Seven Temples after TR. 11 (scale 1:2,500).

FIGURE 2

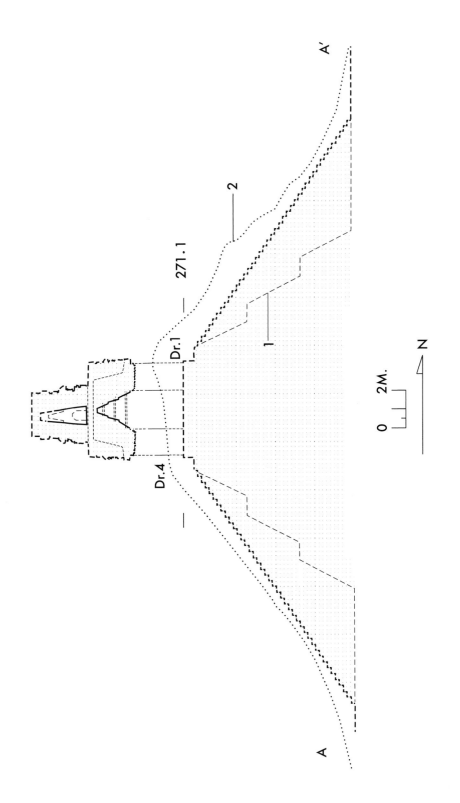

Str. 5D-91 Section/Profile A-A' (scale 1:200).
1, Estimated terrace profile. *2*, Debris line.

FIGURE 3

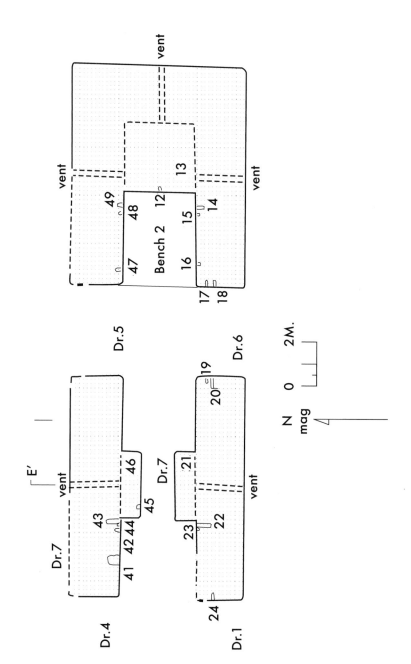

Str. 5D-91 E Half Building Plan (scale 1:100).
12, Miscellaneous wall-hole 2. *13*, Secondary end-wall. *14*, Ss. Bm. 1. *15*, Ss. Bm. 2. *16*, Ss. Bm. 3. *17*, Dr. Bm. 1. *18*, Dr. Bm. 2. *19*, Dr. Bm. 1. *20*, Dr. Bm. 2. *21*, Secondary partition. *22*, Ss. Bm. 6. *23*, Ss. Bm. 4. *24*, Dr. Bm. 3. *41*, Miscella-neous wall-hole 5. *42*, Miscellaneous wall-hole 6. *43*, Ss. Bm. 4. *44*, Ss. Bm. 6. *45*, Miscellaneous wall-hole 7. *46*, Secondary partition. *47*, Ss. Bm. 3. *48*, Ss. Bm. 2. *49*, Ss. Bm. 1.

FIGURE 4

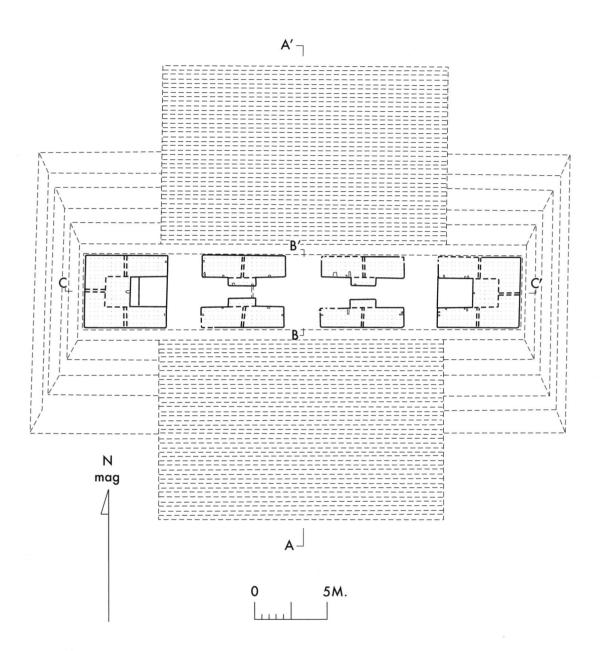

Str. 5D-91 Plan (scale 1:250).
For building details see Fig. 29–32.

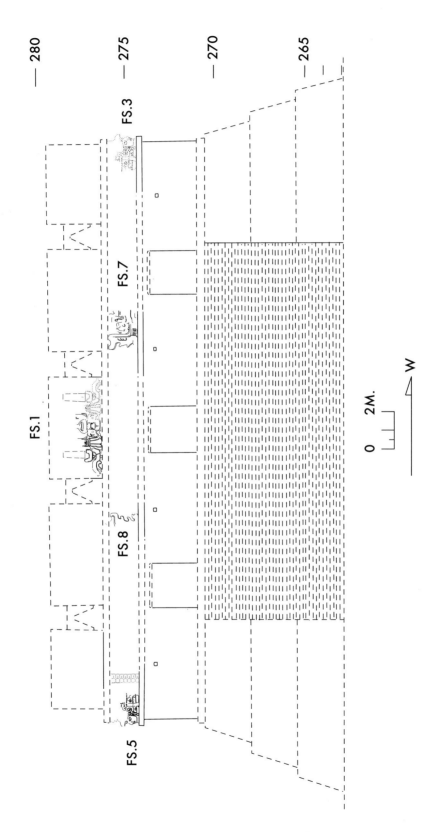

FIGURE 5

Str. 5D-91 N Elevation (scale 1:200).
Terracing conjectural.

FIGURE 6

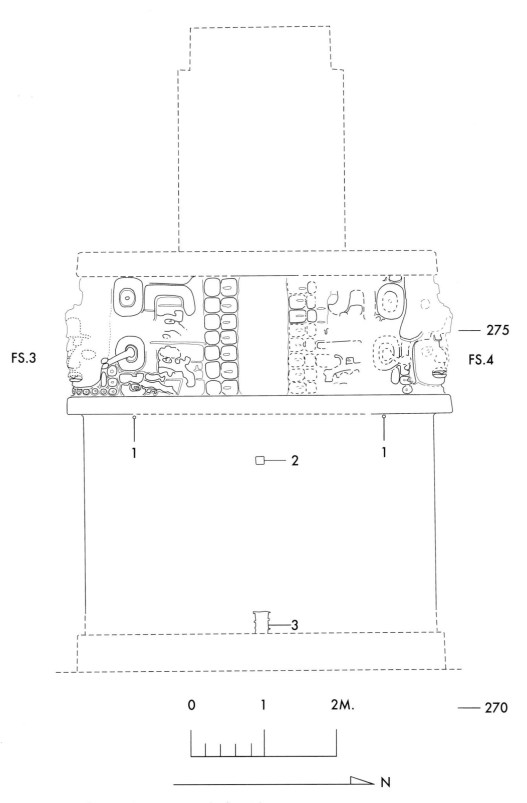

— 280

— 275

FS.3

FS.4

1

2

1

3

0   1   2M.

— 270

N

Str. 5D-91 E Elevation Superstructure (scale 1:50).
1, Rod-row hole. *2*, Vent. *3*, Scaffolding hole.

FIGURE 7

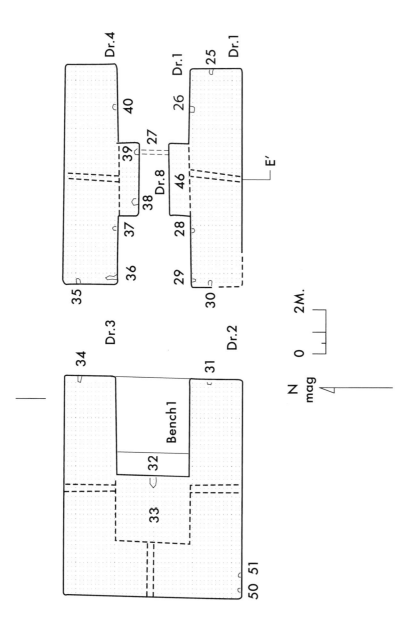

Structure 5D-91 W Half Building Plan (scale 1:100).
25, Dr. Bm. 3. *26*, Ss. Bm. 7. *27*, Secondary seal to Dr. 8. *28*, Ss. Bm. 5. *29*, Ss. Bm. 8. *30*, Dr. Bm. 4. *31*, Dr. Bm. 4. *32*, Miscellaneous wall-hole 3. *33*, Secondary end-wall unit. *34*, Dr. Bm. 5. *35*, Dr. Bm. 5. *36*, Ss. Bm. 8. *37*, Ss. Bm. 5. *38*, Miscellaneous wall-hole 4. *39*, Dr. Bm. 6. *40*, Ss. Bm. 7. *50*, Miscellaneous wall-hole 8. *51*, Miscellaneous wall-hole 9.

FIGURE 8

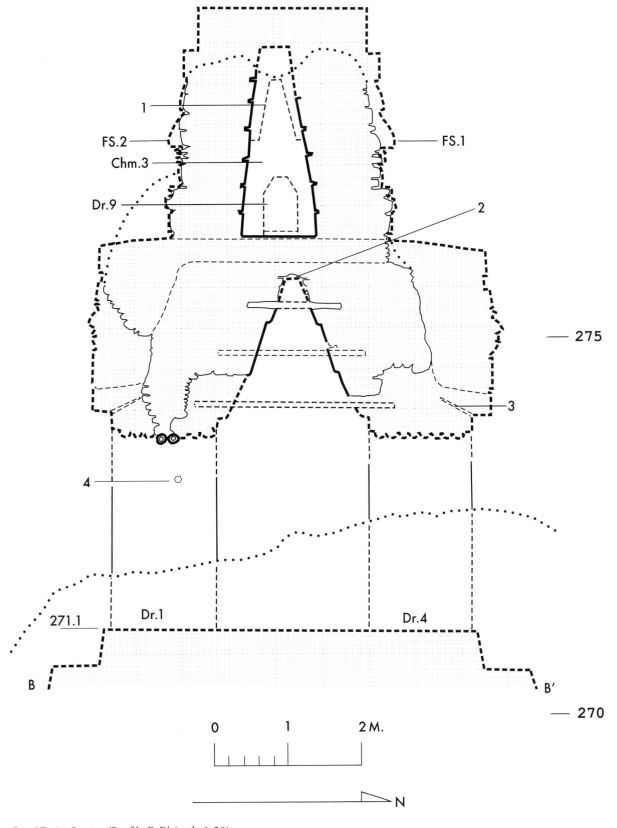

Str. 5D-91 Section/Profile B-B' (scale 1:50).
1, Shoulder-vault unit. *2*, Preplastered capstone. *3*, Rod-row socket. *4*, Dr. Bm. 25.

FIGURE 9

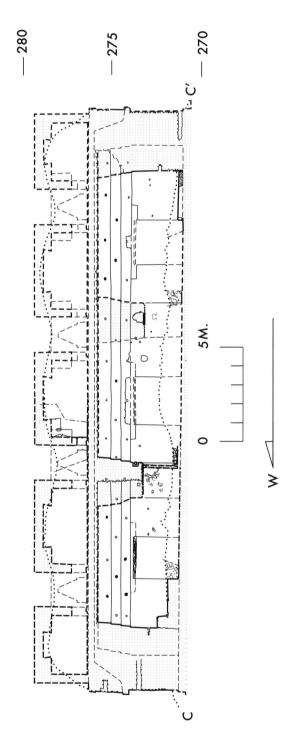

Str. 5D-91 Section/Profile C-C' (scale 1:200).

FIGURE 10

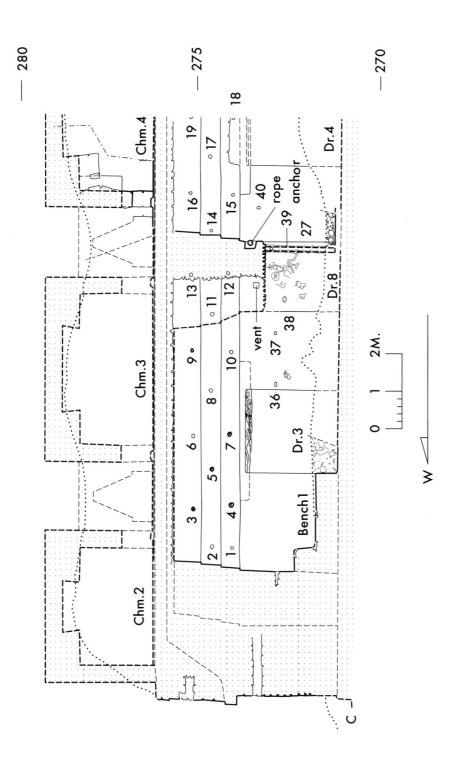

Str. 5D-91 W Half Section C-C' (scale 1:100).
1–18, Vault beams. 27, Secondary seal to Dr. 8. 36, Ss. Bm. 8. 37, Ss. Bm. 5. 38, Miscellaneous wall-hole 4. 39, Dr. Bm. 6. 40, Ss. Bm. 7.

FIGURE 11

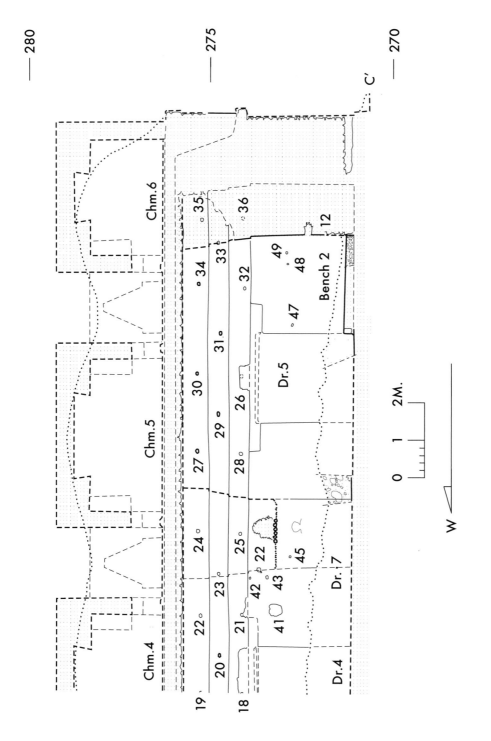

Str. 5D-91 E Half Section C-C′ (scale 1:100).
12, Miscellaneous wall-hole 2. *19–36*, Vault-beam holes. *41*, Miscellaneous wall-hole 5. *42*, Miscellaneous wall-hole 6. *43*, Ss. Bm. 4.
45, Miscellaneous wall-hole 7. *47*, Ss. Bm. 3. *48*, Ss. Bm. 2. *49*, Ss. Bm. 1.

FIGURE 12

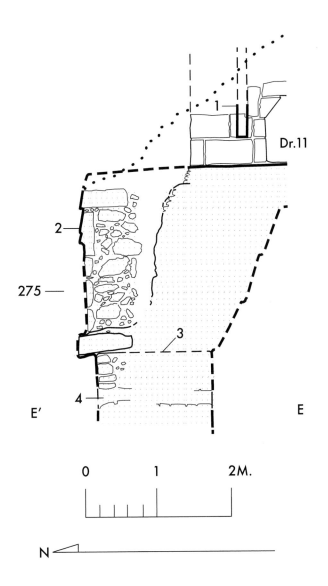

Str. 5D-91 Section/Profile E-E' (scale 1:50).
1, Arch screen. *2*, Part of facade sculpture 8. *3*, Plastered
wall top. *4*, Vent.

FIGURE 13

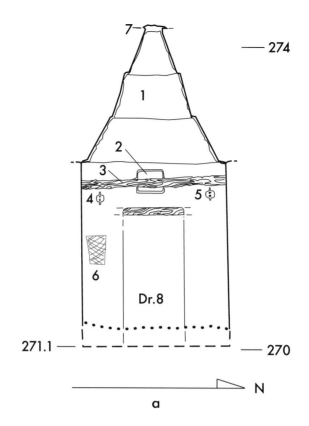

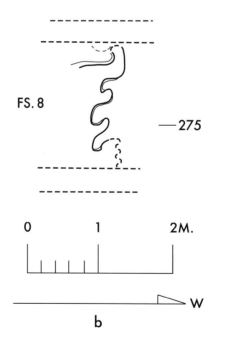

Str. 5D-91 Details (scale 1:50).
a. E elevation Dr. 8. *1*, Fake-vault of secondary partition.
2, Rope anchor. *3*, Ss. Bm. 8. *4*, Cord holder. *5*, Cord
holder. *6*, Graffito. *b*. Facade sculpture 8.

FIGURE 14

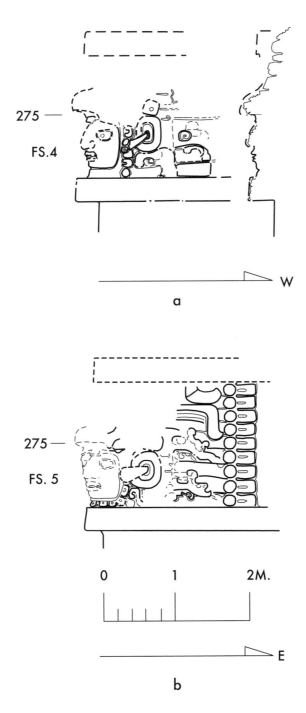

275 —

FS.4

W

a

275 —

FS. 5

0   1   2M.

E

b

Str. 5D-91 Facade Sculpture (scale 1:50).
a. Facade sculpture 4, profile on corner diagonal.
b. Facade sculpture 5.

FIGURE 15

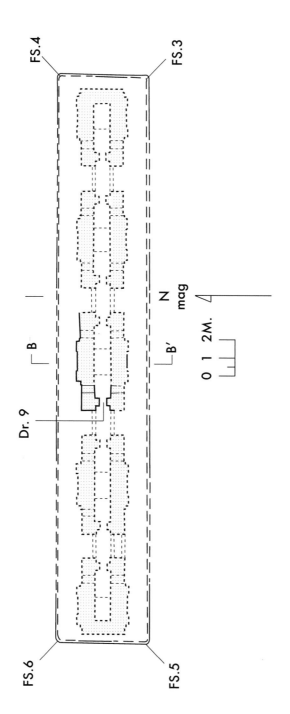

Structure 5D-91 Roof Structure Plan (scale 1:200).

FIGURE 16

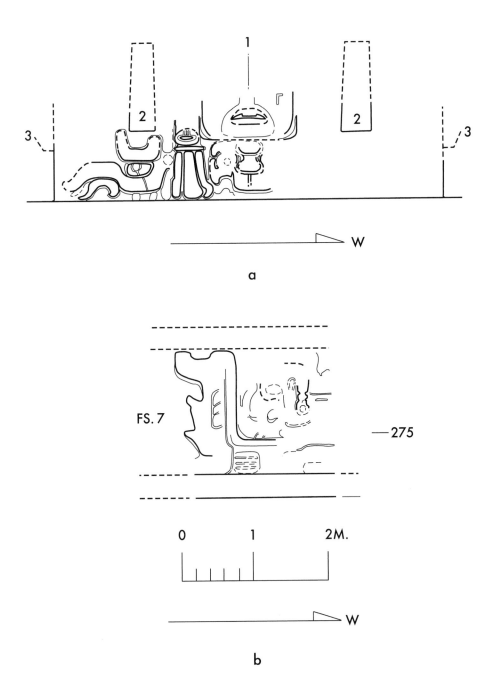

Structure 5D-91 Facade Sculpture (scale 1:50).
a. 1, Human face. *2*, Window. *3*, Arch screen. *b*. Facade Sculpture 7.

FIGURE 17

a

b

Str. 5D-91 Photographs.
a. Dr. 7 looking E. *b*. N facade Dr. 4 and vault-back.

FIGURE 18

a

b

Str. 5D-91 Photographs.
a. NE corner, facade sculpture 4. *b*. Facade sculpture 4, E facade.

FIGURE 19

a

b

Str. 5D-91 Photographs.
a. Facade sculpture 3, NW corner. *b*. Facade sculpture 3.

FIGURE 20

a

b

Str. 5D-91 Photographs.
a. View of Dr. 8. *b*. E end interior, Bench 1.

FIGURE 21

a

b

Str. 5D-91 Photographs.
a. Roof-structure Dr. 9. *b*. View of Str. 5D-91 looking SE.

FIGURE 22

a

b

Str. 5D-92 Photographs.
a. View of N face. *b*. View of S face.

FIGURE 23

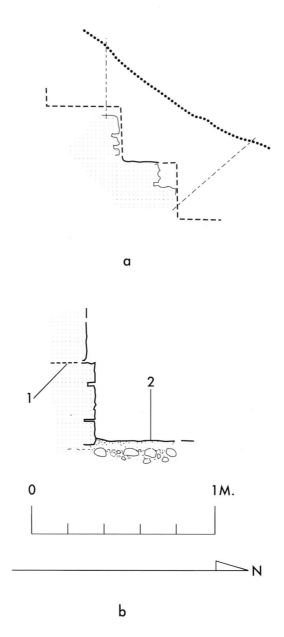

a

b

Str. 5D-92 Details (scale 1:20).
a. Stair detail. *b*. Building Platform detail. *1*, Plaster
surface. *2*, Plaster terrace top.

FIGURE 24

a

b

Structure 5D-92 Photographs.
a. View of E facade. *b*. View of S facade W end.

FIGURE 25

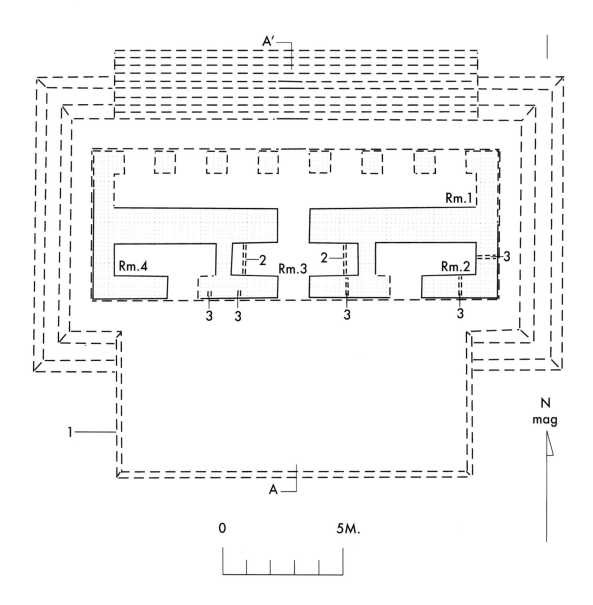

Str. 5D-92 Plan (scale 1:125).
1, Conjectural upper-zone outline. *2*, Extant subspring beam. *3*, Scaffolding hole.

FIGURE 26

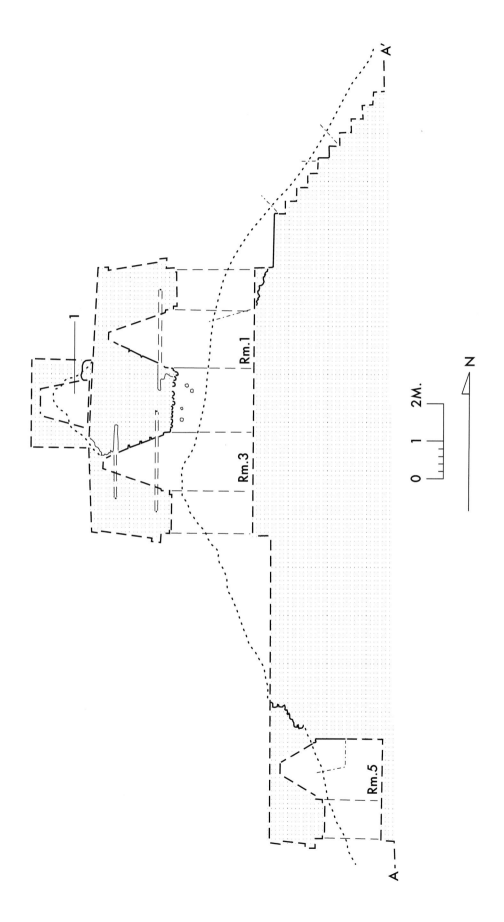

Str. 5D-92 Section/Profile A-A' (scale 1:100).
1, Roof structure chamber.

Str. 5D-92 Details.
a. Part axial section/profile at spine wall (scale 1:50). *1*, Floor associated with roof structures.
2, Roof surface. *3*, Level of lintel bed. *4*, Level of lintel bed. *5*, Plugged and sealed jamb hole.
6, Debris surface. *7*, Estimated floor level. *8*, Empty jamb hole. *b*. View of Rm. 3 W end.

FIGURE 27

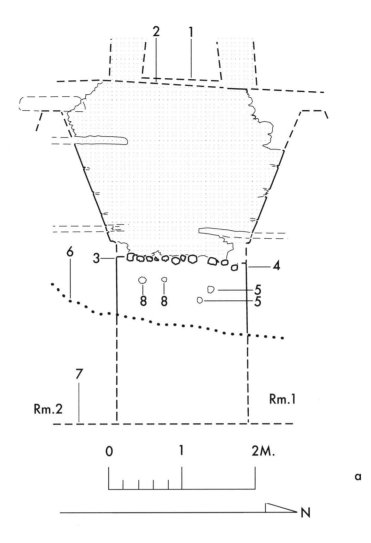

a

b

FIGURE 28

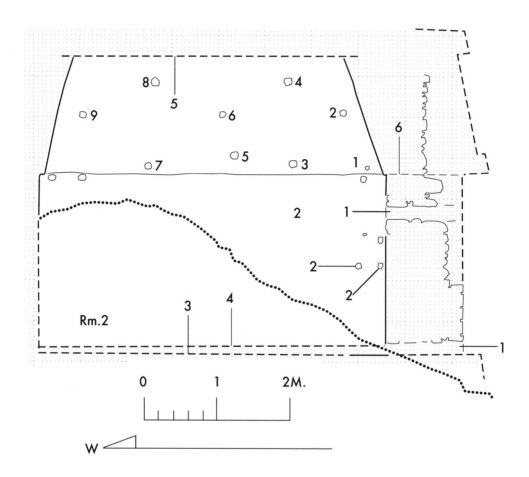

Str. 5D-92 N Elevation Rm. 2 (scale 1:50).
1, Scaffolding hole. *2*, Plugged hole. *3*, Fl. 1. *4*, Fl. 2. *5*, Preplastered capstones. *6*, Plastered wall top. *1–9*, Vault-beam holes in roof area.

FIGURE 29

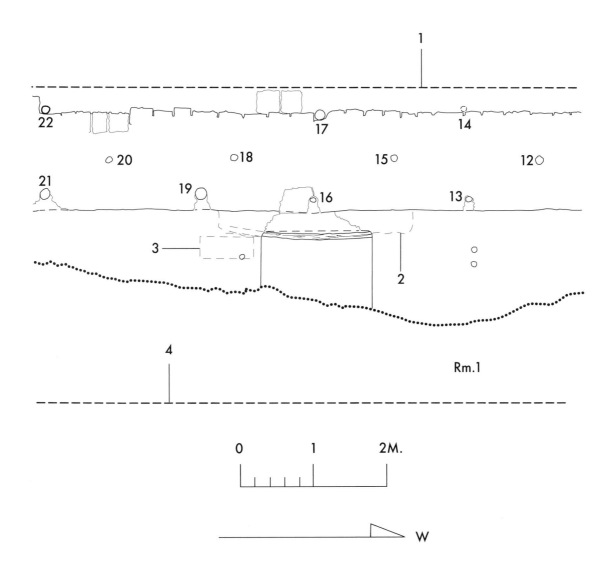

Str. 5D-92 S Elevation Central Part Rm. 1 (scale 1:50).
1, Estimated level of roof. *2*, Lintel bed. *3*, Sealed feature (niche?). *4*, Estimated floor level.
12–22, Vault beam holes.

FIGURE 30

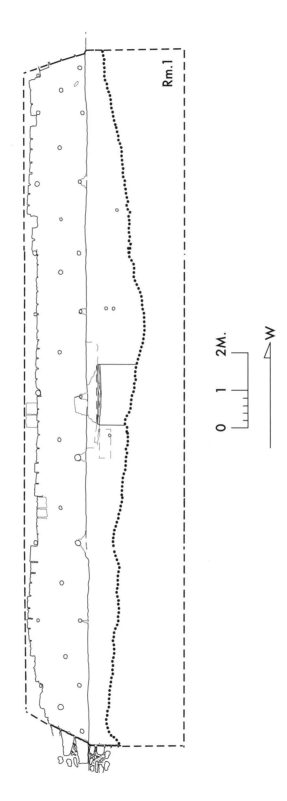

Str. 5D-92 S Elevation Rm. 1 (scale 1:50).

FIGURE 31

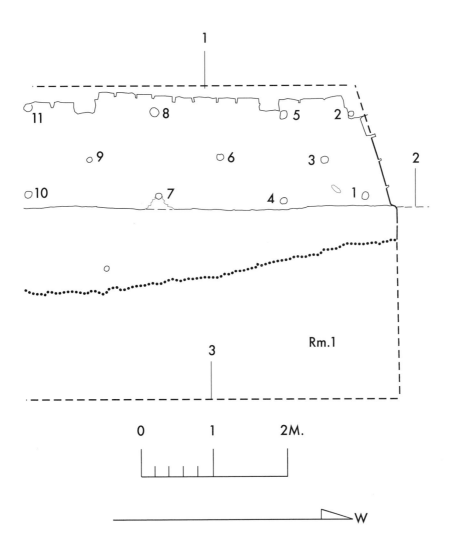

Str. 5D-92 S Elevation W Part Rm. 1 (scale 1:50).
1, Estimated capstone level. *2*, Plastered wall top. *3*, Estimated floor level.
1–11, Vault beam holes.

FIGURE 32

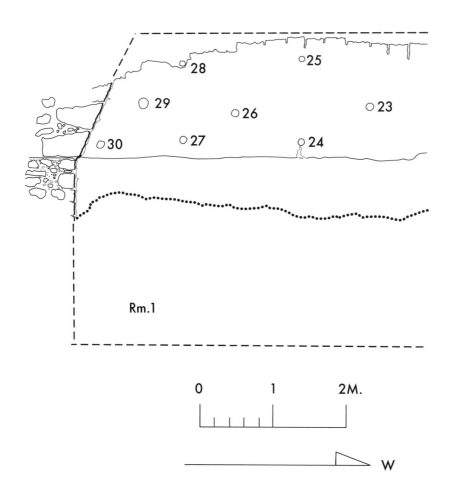

Str. 5D-92 S Elevation E Part Rm. 1.
23–30, Vault beam holes.

FIGURE 33

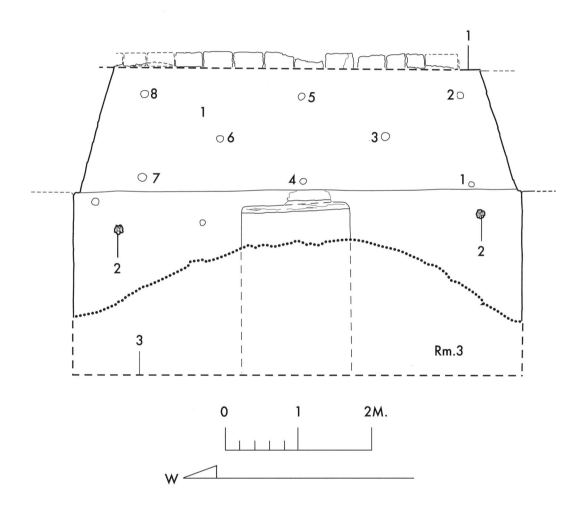

Str. 5D-92 N Elevation Rm. 3 (scale 1:50).
1, Preplastered capstones. *2*, Subspring beam. *3*, Estimated floor level.
1–8, Vault beam holes.

FIGURE 34

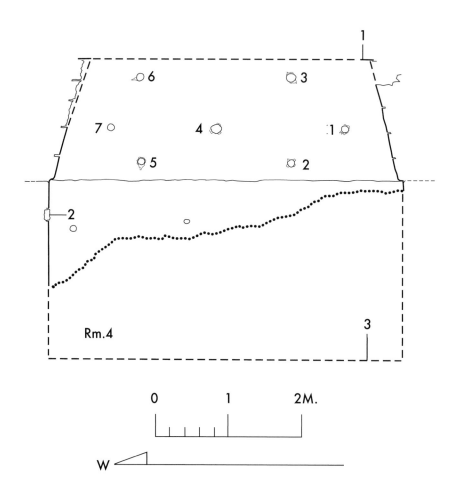

Str. 5D-92 N Elevation Rm. 4 (scale 1:50).
1, Preplastered capstones. *2*, Plugged hole. *3*, Estimated floor level.
1–7, Vault beam holes.

FIGURE 35

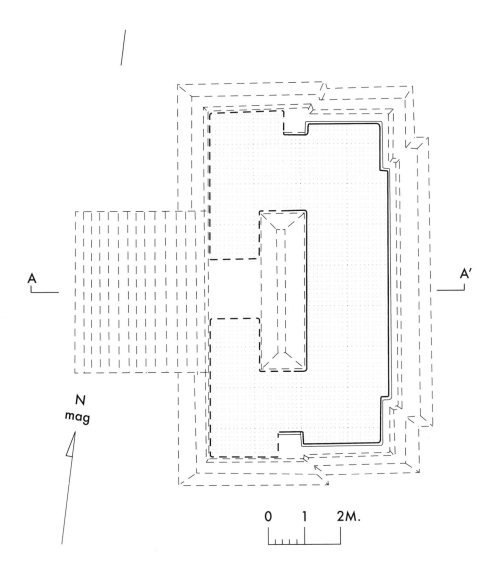

A

A′

N
mag

0   1   2M.

Str. 5D-93 Plan (scale 1:100).

FIGURE 36

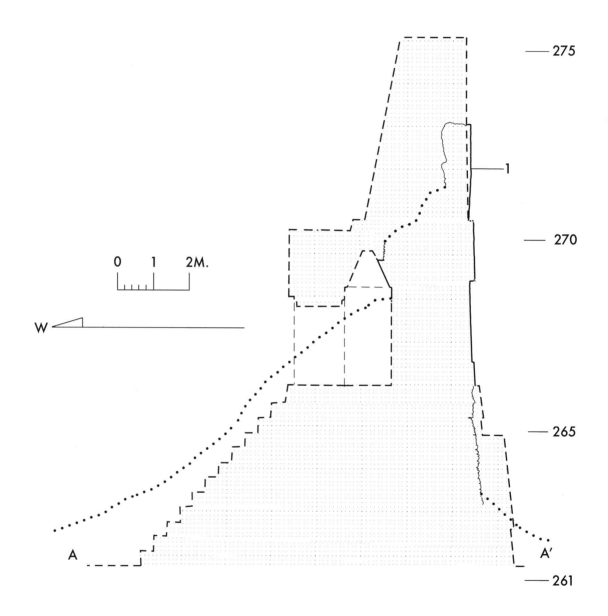

Str. 5D-93 Section/Profile A-A' (scale 1:100).
1, Displaced rear roofcomb facing.

FIGURE 37

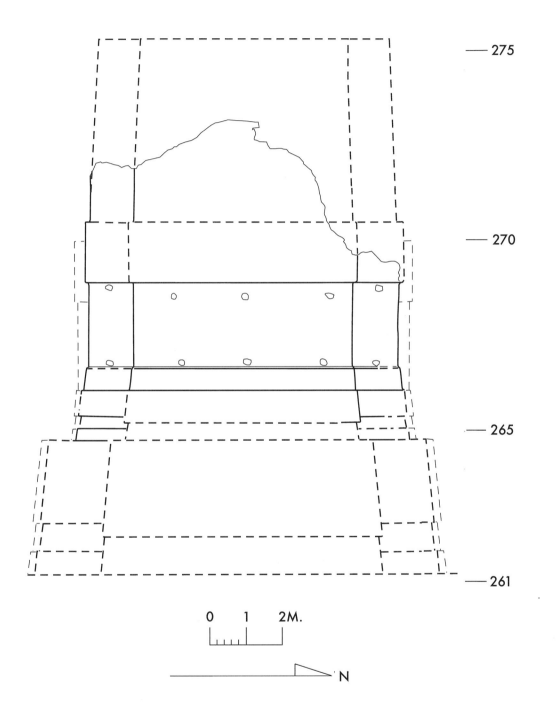

— 275

— 270

— 265

— 261

0   1   2M.

N

Str. 5D-93 E Elevation (scale 1:100).

FIGURE 38

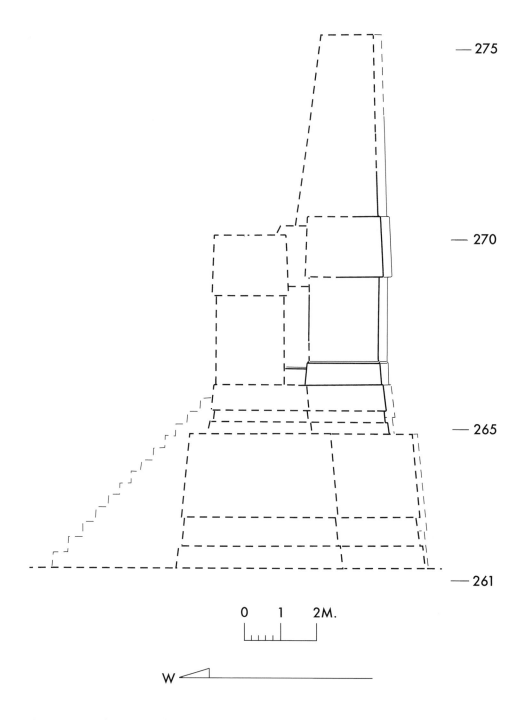

Str. 5D-93 S Elevation (scale 1:100).

FIGURE 39

Str. 5D-93 View of E Facade.

FIGURE 40

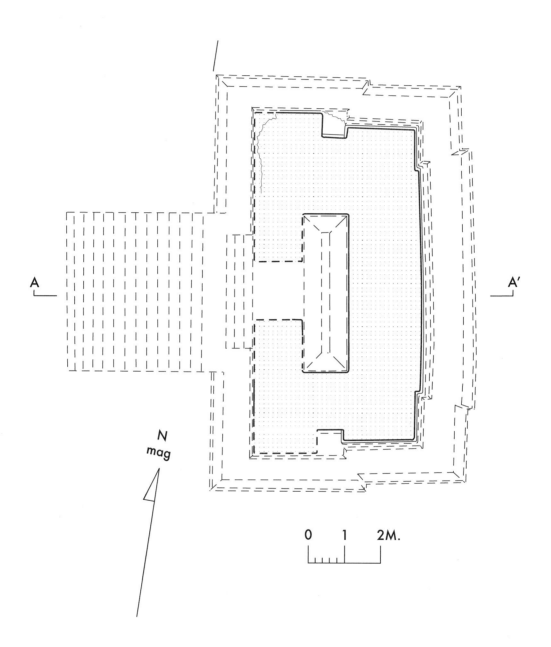

A   A'

N
mag

0   1   2M.

Str. 5D-94 Plan (scale 1:100).

FIGURE 41

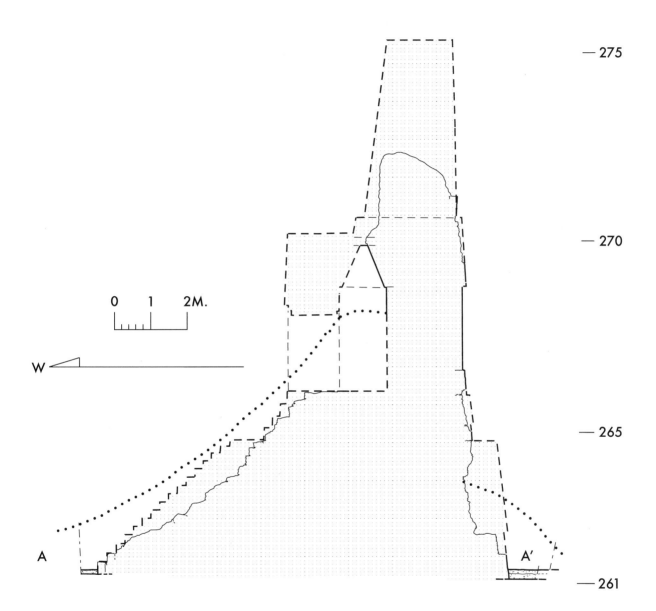

— 275

— 270

0   1   2M.

W

— 265

A   A'

— 261

Str. 5D-94 Section/Profile A-A' (scale 1:100).

FIGURE 42

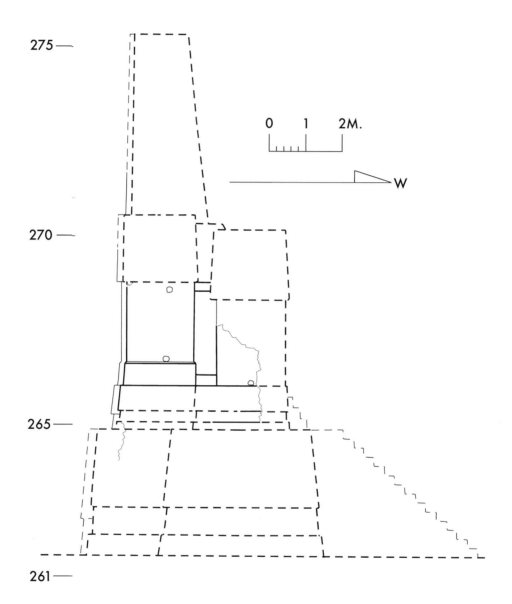

275 —

270 —

265 —

261 —

0   1   2M.

W

Str. 5D-94 N Elevation (scale 1:100).

FIGURE 43

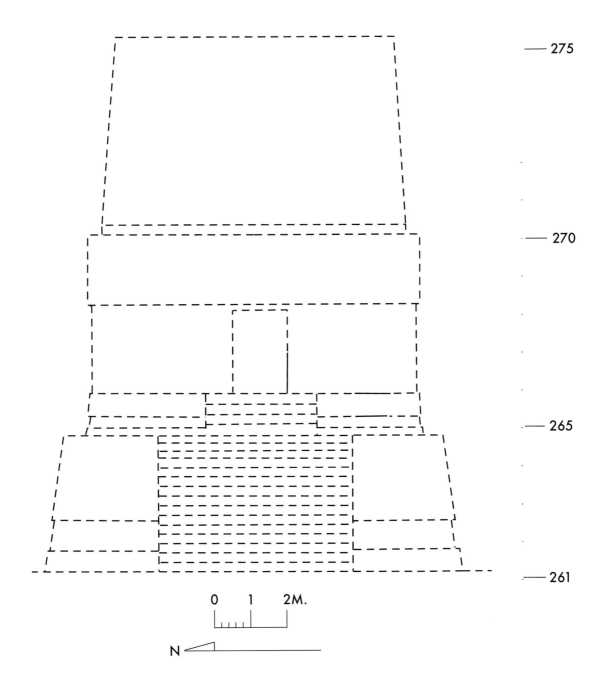

—— 275

—— 270

—— 265

—— 261

0   1   2M.

N

Str. 5D-94 W Elevation (scale 1:100).

FIGURE 44

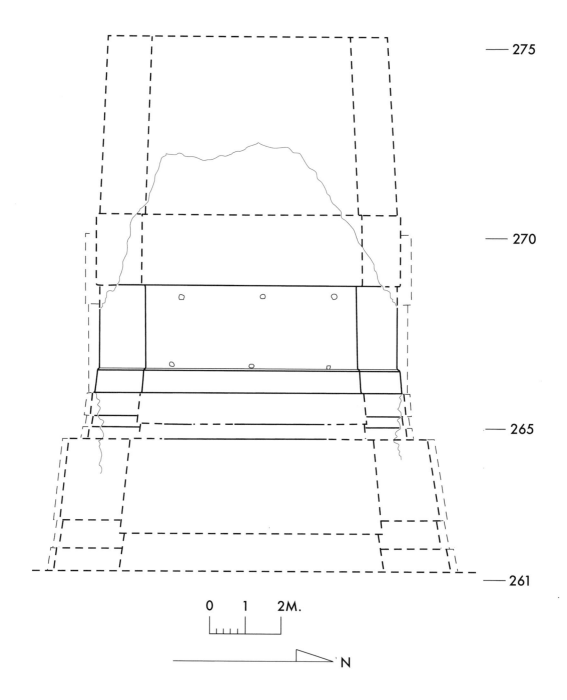

—275

—270

—265

—261

0 1 2M.

N

Str. 5D-94 E Elevation (scale 1:100).

FIGURE 45

a

b

Str. 5D-94 Photographs.
a. View of E facade. *b*. View of NE corner.

FIGURE 46

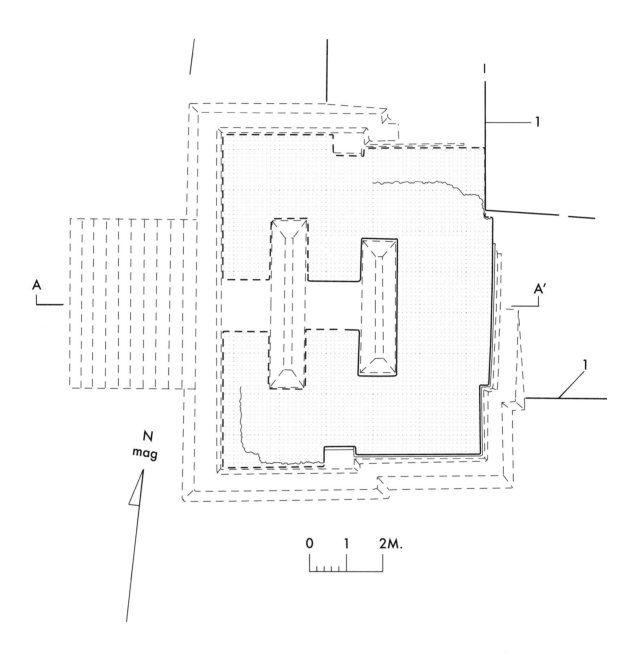

Str. 5D-95 Plan (scale 1:100).
1, Top edge of South Acropolis platform.

FIGURE 47

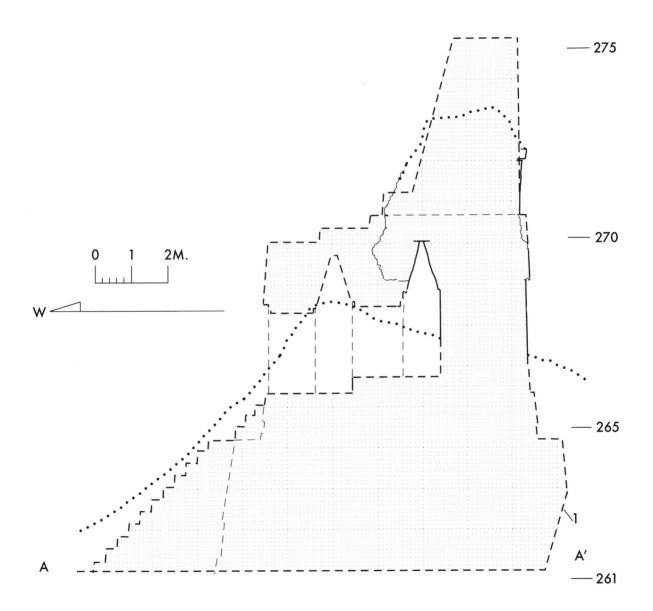

— 275

— 270

— 265

1

A′

— 261

Str. 5D-95 Section/Profile A-A' (scale 1:100).
1, Estimated line of South Acropolis platform.

FIGURE 48

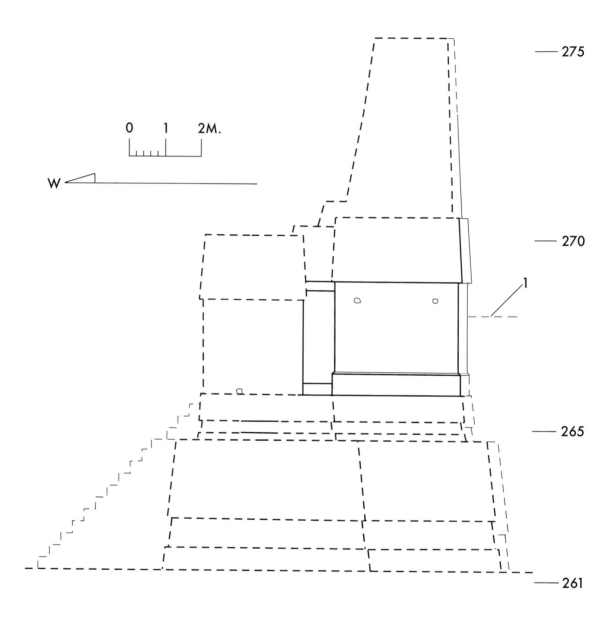

Str. 5D-95 S Elevation (scale 1:100).
1, Top of South Acropolis platform.

FIGURE 49

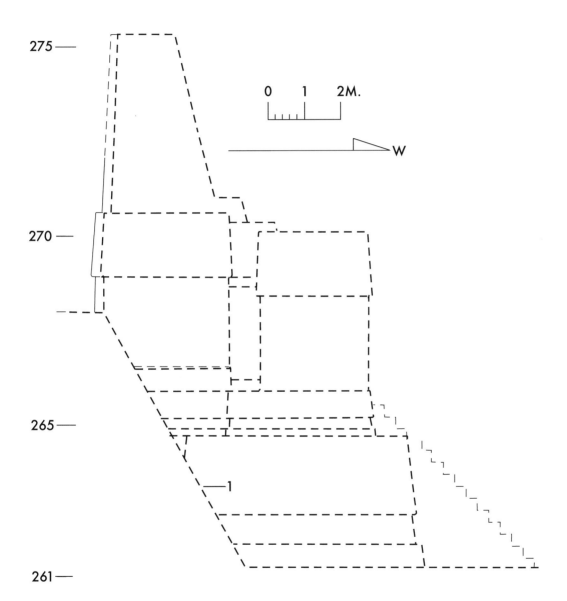

Str. 5D-95 N Elevation (scale 1:100).
1, Estimated face of South Acropolis platform.

FIGURE 50

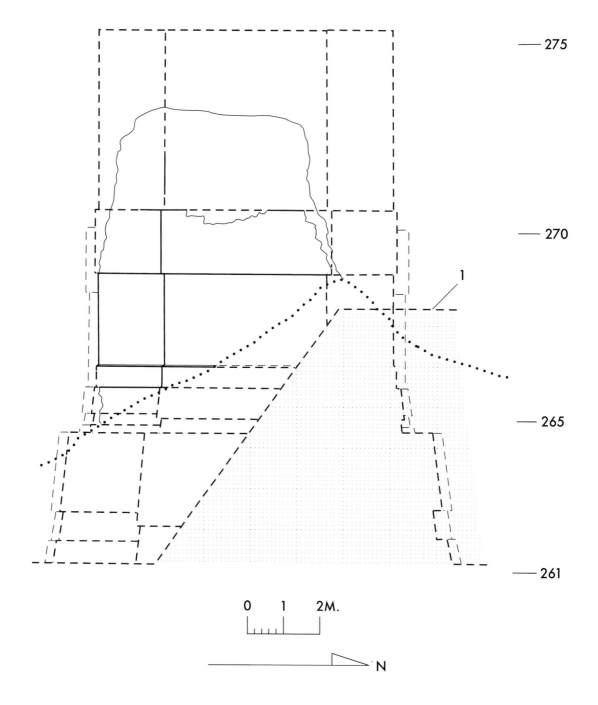

— 275

— 270

— 265

— 261

1

0   1   2M.

N

Str. 5D-95 E Elevation (scale 1:100).
1, Estimated surface of South Acropolis platform.

FIGURE 51

Str. 5D-95 View Looking SW.

FIGURE 52

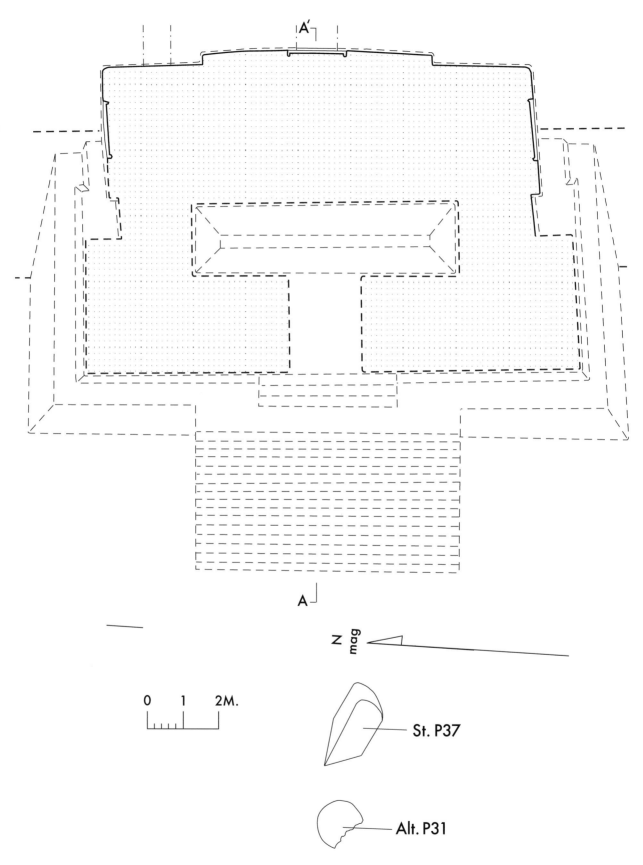

A′

N mag

0   1   2M.

St. P37

Alt. P31

Str. 5D-96 Plan (scale 1:100).

FIGURE 53

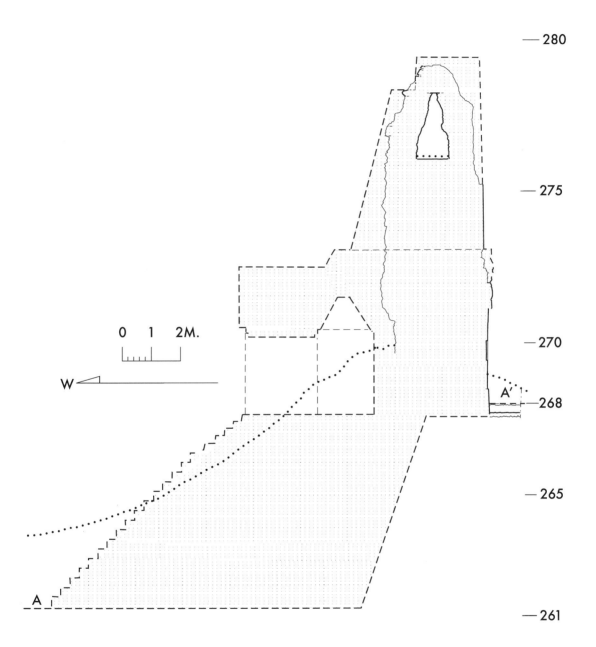

—280

—275

—270

—268

—265

—261

A'

A

W

0 1 2M.

Str. 5D-96 Section/Profile A-A' (scale 1:120).

FIGURE 54

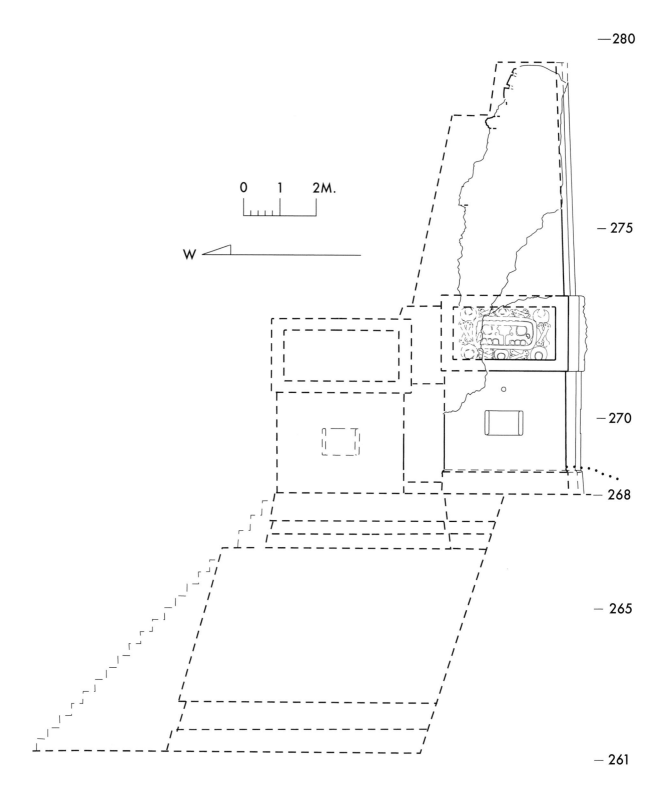

—280

—275

—270

—268

—265

—261

0   1   2M.

W

Str. 5D-96 S Elevation (scale 1:100).

FIGURE 55

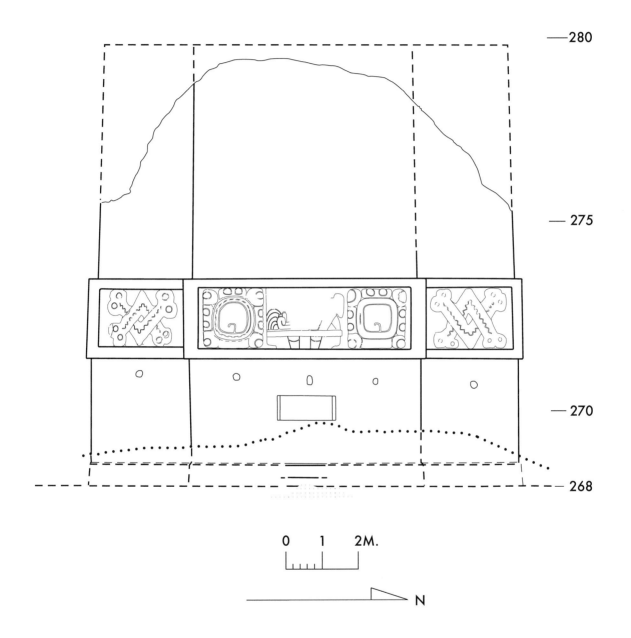

Str. 5D-96 E Elevation (scale 1:100).

FIGURE 56

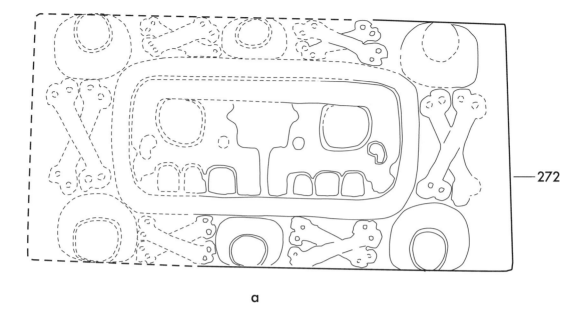

272

a

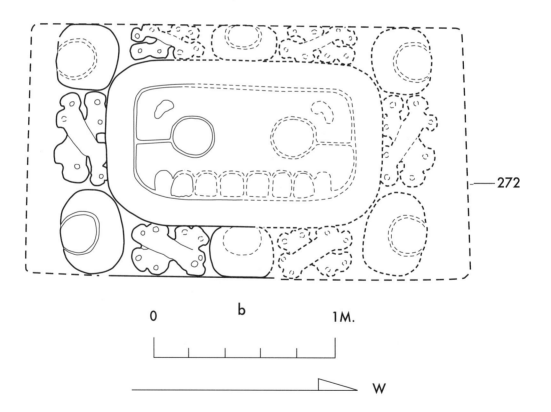

272

0   b   1M.

W

Str. 5D-96 Relief Sculpture (scale 1:20).
a. Upper-zone N panel. *b*. Upper-zone S panel.

FIGURE 57

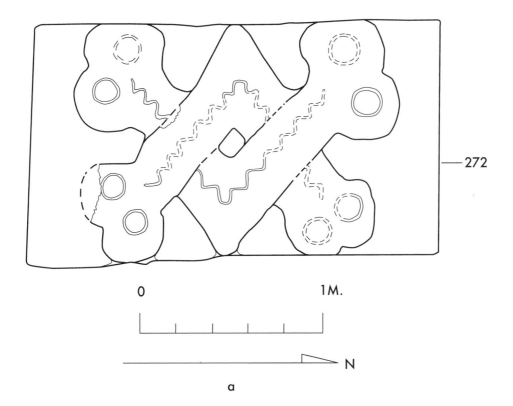

272

0   1M.

N

a

b

Str. 5D-96 Relief Sculpture.
a. S panel upper-zone E facade (scale 1:20). *b.* S panel upper-zone E facade.

FIGURE 58

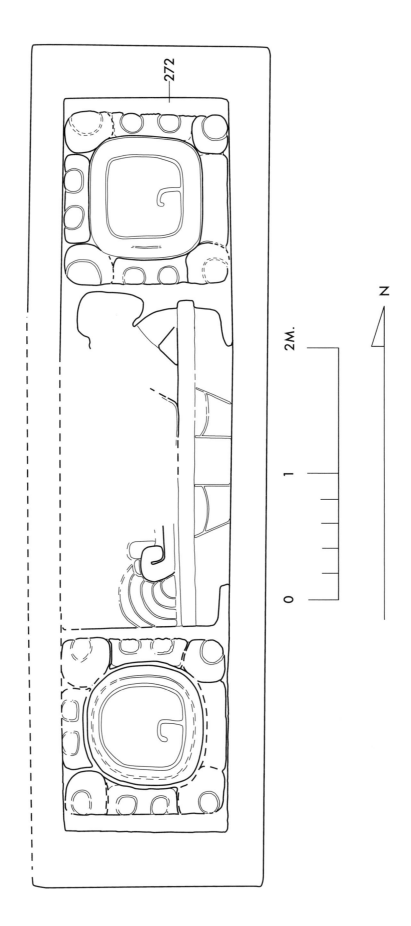

Str. 5D-96 Upper-Zone E Facade Central Panel (scale 1:30).

FIGURE 59

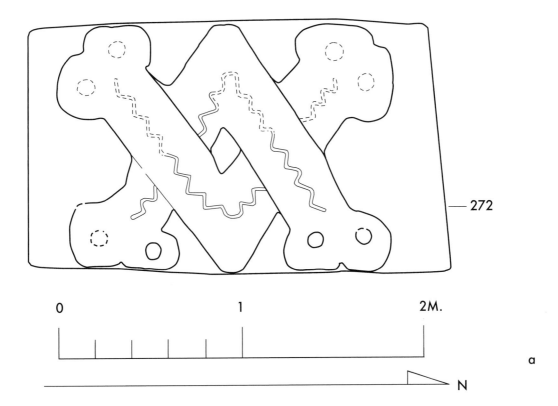

272

0   1   2M.

N

a

b

Str. 5D-96 Relief Sculpture.
a. N panel E facade (scale 1:20). *b*. S motif central panel E facade.

FIGURE 60

a

b

Str. 5D-96 Photographs.
a. View looking SW. *b*. View looking NW.

FIGURE 61

Str. 5D-96 View of E Facade.

FIGURE 62

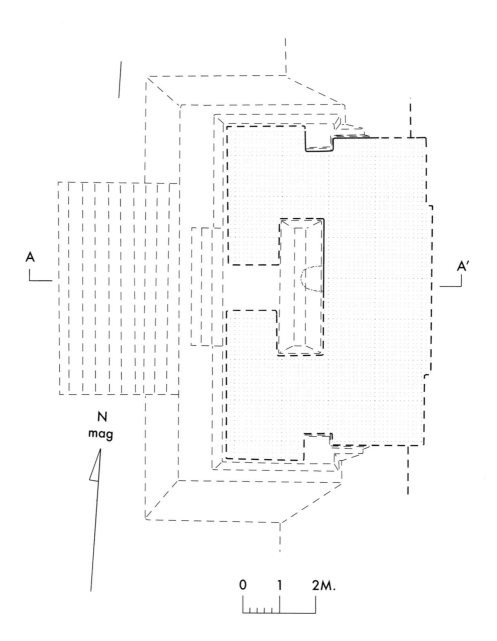

Str. 5D-97 Plan (scale 1:100).

FIGURE 63

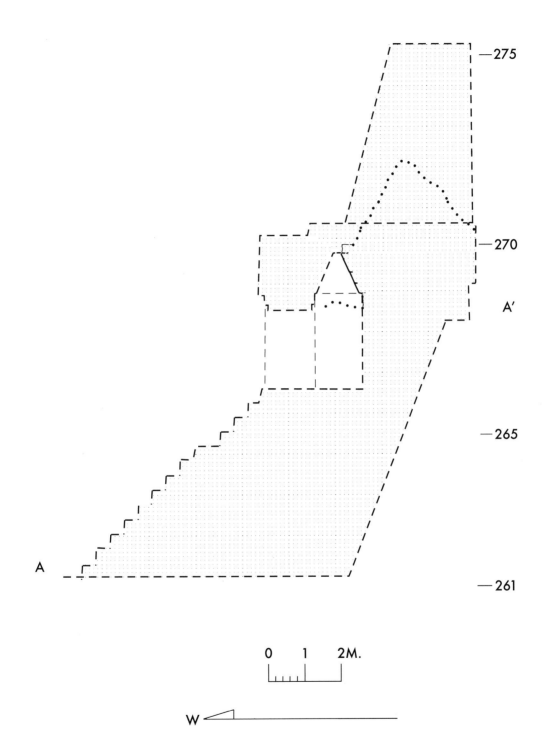

—275

—270

A'

—265

—261

0 1 2M.

W

Str. 5D-97 Section/Profile A-A' (scale 1:100).

FIGURE 64

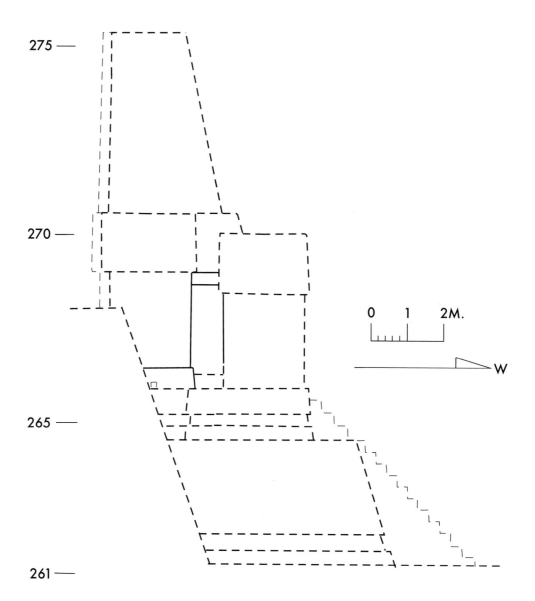

275 —

270 —

265 —

261 —

0   1   2M.

W

Str. 5D-97 N Elevation (scale 1:100).

FIGURE 65

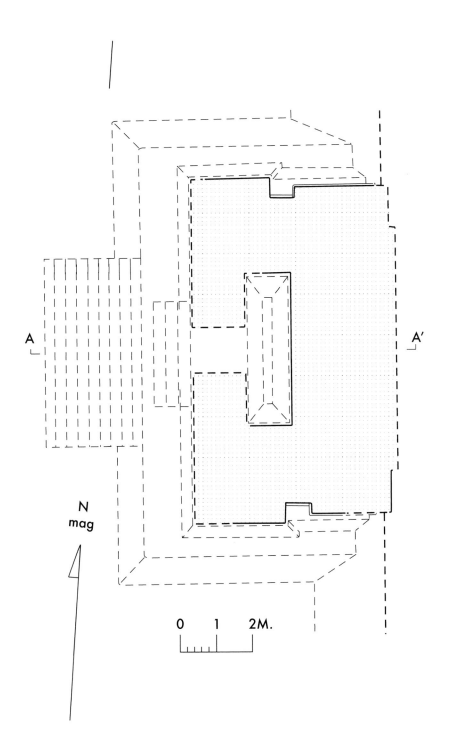

A   A′

N
mag

0   1   2M.

Str. 5D-98 Plan (scale 1:100).

FIGURE 66

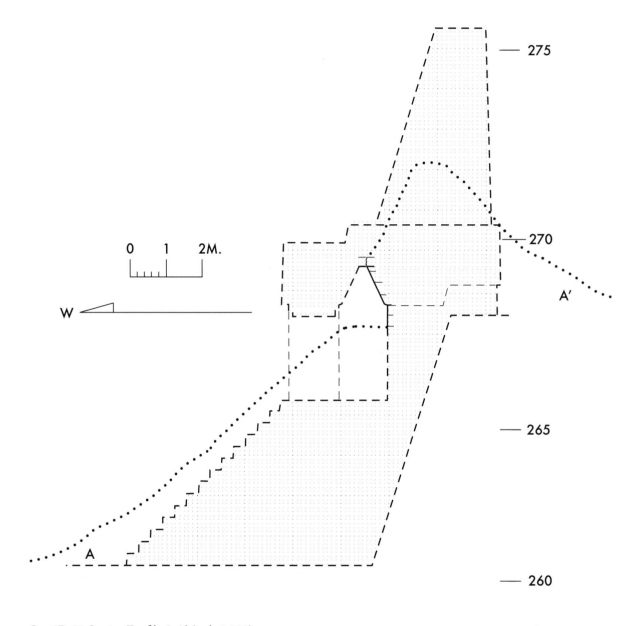

Str. 5D-98 Section/Profile A-A' (scale 1:100).

FIGURE 67

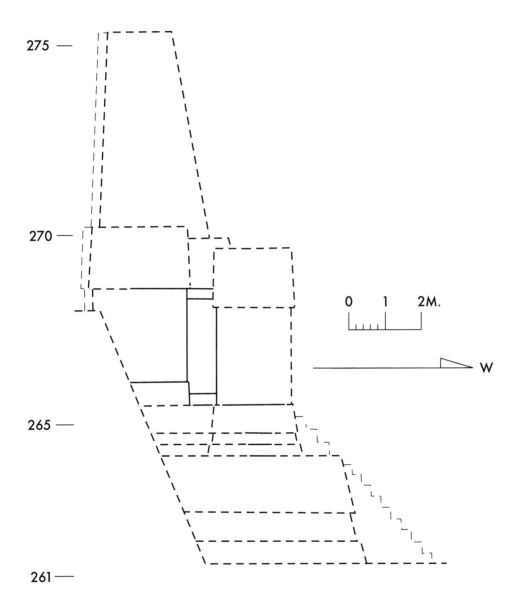

275 —

270 —

265 —

261 —

0   1   2M.

W

Str. 5D-98 N Elevation (scale 1:100).

FIGURE 68

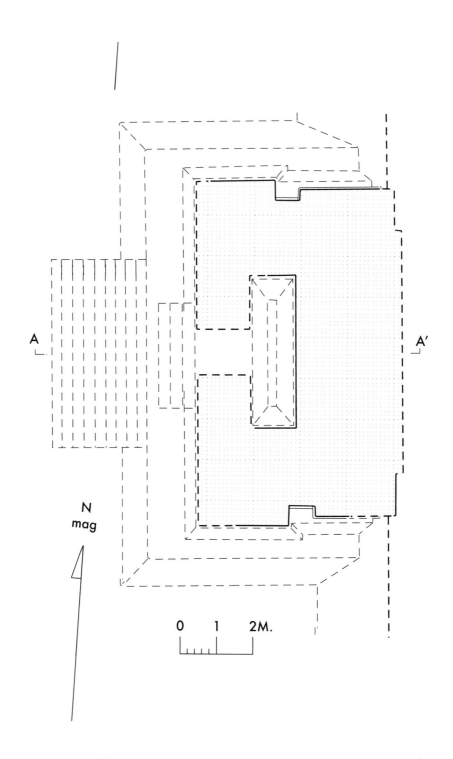

A   A′

N
mag

0   1   2M.

Str. 5D-99 Plan (scale 1:100).

FIGURE 69

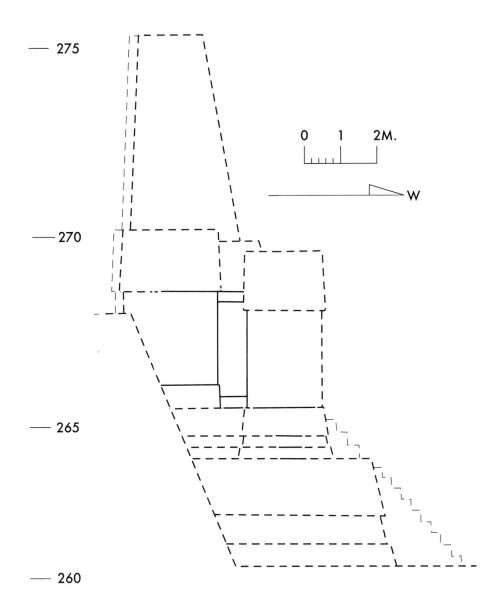

Str. 5D-99 N Elevation (scale 1:100).